VATICAN OBSERVED

Vatican Observed

AN ANGLICAN IMPRESSION OF VATICAN II

John Moorman BISHOP OF RIPON

LONDON
DARTON, LONGMAN & TODD

First published in 1967 by
Darton, Longman & Todd Ltd,
64 Chiswick High Road, London W.4
© 1967 John Moorman
Printed in Great Britain by
The Bowering Press Plymouth

CONTENTS

CHAPTER ONE

A Time to Sew

THE HOLDING OF THE SECOND VATICAN COUNCIL
means that, for the first time since 1439, we can begin to think
and talk about Christian Unity. The Council of Florence, in
that year, engineered some kind of patched-up union between
East and West, so healing a schism which had lasted, with one
brief interval, for 385 years. But the union did not last. Within
a few years the breach had reopened, the two parts of the
Christian Church slid apart again, and have remained so ever
since. Then, within a few years, came the disintegration of the
Western Church, and the multiplication of independent and
often mutually hostile Churches and sects, so that the seamless
robe of Christ, the ancient symbol of unity, has been rent into a
large number of pieces – some large, some small, but all
separated from each other.

'There is', says the Preacher, 'a time to every purpose under
the heaven . . . a time to rend and a time to sew.'[1] It is on the
basis of this that divisions have taken place. Christians have
separated from each other because they were convinced that it
was the *right* thing to do. In the eleventh century the Churches
of East and West thought it *right* that each should go its own
way. In the sixteenth century the reformers thought the Church

[1] *Ecclesiastes* 3: 1, 7.

so corrupt that it was *right* that they should break away from it·
In the eighteenth and nineteenth centuries the followers of John
Wesley thought it *right* that they should sever their connection
with the Anglican Church. It was all very sad, but there was no
choice. God was calling them, and they must obey.

It was, therefore, 'a time to rend'. But everyone agrees that
we are now living at a moment when it is 'a time to sew'. The
condition of mankind today and the cause of Christ both
demand that Christians should present a united front. The
whole of Christendom is, therefore, committed to a search for
Unity.

With the exception of the Roman Catholic Church, all other
Churches have been engaged in the search for Unity – or, at
least, for a union of such Churches as were willing to join in –
for some time. But in all these ecumenical conversations and
negotiations the Church of Rome has held aloof. She has done
so because her attitude towards Christian Unity has been very
different from that of other Churches. To her there is really no
problem at all. The Unity for which Christ prayed already exists
in the Church which he founded and over which the successor
of S. Peter presides. Cardinal Bea has put this both clearly and
charitably. Writing on 'How the Catholic Church understands
the ecumenical movement', he says:

> 'Briefly it can be set out in three propositions. The first: that
> essential unity already exists in the Catholic Church and is the
> unity which Christ willed and achieved in Peter and his successors,
> the bishops of Rome: unity of doctrine, sacraments and rule. The
> second: that there is a further unity still to be achieved, the unity
> of the members unhappily separated from the Apostolic See. The
> third: that this unity of the separated members is not to be brought
> about by force, but by the free acceptance of union with the
> Catholic Church, it being "absolutely necessary that this should
> come about by their free choice, since no man believes unless he is
> willing". We must, then, help to prepare for it by patient labour,
> full of understanding and charity, according to the capacity of

each son of the Church. In the last analysis, it will be the work of
the Holy Ghost, for he alone can give separated brethren light
and strength to overcome all the difficulties which delay the
decisive step.'[1]

By 'the decisive step' he means, of course, submission to Rome.

This self-confidence and intransigence forms a barrier of the
greatest magnitude which we must not minimise or ignore. We
come up against it in whatever direction we look – sometimes as
a soft but impenetrable curtain, sometimes as a stone wall.
'The Catholic Church', said Fr Ciappi on the eve of the Second
Vatican Council, 'has everything to give and nothing to receive.
The depositum of divine truth and the means of sanctification
repose, in their entirety, in her alone.'[2] This puts it bluntly
enough; but Pope John was really taking the same line when he
saw himself as a loving father calling his prodigal sons to come
home again. 'Let us,' he said, addressing the separated brethren,
'let us call you sons and brothers. Allow us in our fatherly and
loving heart to cherish the hope for your return. . . . Observe,
we beg of you, that when we lovingly invite you to the unity of
the Church, we are inviting you not to the home of a stranger,
but to your own, your Father's house.' (*Ad Petri cathedram*,
1959).

If the Roman Catholic Church really thought it had 'everything to give and nothing to receive', there was obviously no
point in its members taking part in ecumenical discussions. Indeed, participation in such discussions might give the impression
that the Church of Rome was, in some way, just one among
many denominations. This would never do; and successive
popes had forbidden members of their Church to participate in
any of the conferences which had been held from time to time

[1] Augustine Bea, *The Unity of Christians*, ed. B. Leeming, S.J. (London,
1963), p. 35. The quotation is from Pius XII's encyclical *Mystici
Corporis*.
[2] Quoted by V. Subilia in *The Problem of Catholicity* (London, 1963),
p. 15.

to discuss problems of unity. The encyclical, *Mortalium animos*, of Pius XI in 1928, after the abortive Malines Conversations, and the Instructions issued by the Holy Office in 1948 and 1949 at the time of the formation of the World Council of Churches, had cut Roman Catholics off from any open dialogue with their fellow Christians.[1] The Christian world was, therefore, divided into two more or less equal parts, one half struggling, hoping, praying for Christian Unity, while the other half stood aloof in splendid isolation, inviting the erring sons to return to their Father's house.

In face of all this, the non-Roman half of Christendom had no choice but to go its own way. Most of them thought that it was foolish and futile to bother about Rome, which seemed to them so remote not only from the rest of the Christian world but also from the Christianity of the New Testament that there was no point in having anything to do with her. The 'glorious Reformation' had restored the Christianity of the Bible: Rome had not only failed to do this but had added further dogmas to the Faith, dogmas for which there was no warrant in Holy Scripture. It was not Protestants, but Roman Catholics, who had erred from their Father's house, and needed now to be brought back.

This is the opposite point of view, and is strongly held in large parts of the Christian Church. That members of reformed Churches should have any dealings whatever with Rome seemed to them madness, if not treachery.

'Protestant Churchmen in foreign countries', wrote Bishop George Bell, 'often find it difficult to understand how loyal and intelligent members of the Church of England can conceive it possible to have relations with the Church of Rome. What are called Jesuits in disguise or crypto-Papists *may* (they suppose) capture key posts in the Anglican Church in order in the end to place it under the

[1] G. K. A. Bell, *Documents on Christian Unity: Fourth Series.* (London, 1958), pp. 16–17, 22–7. It is interesting to observe that the Instructions are signed by Alfredo Ottaviani, *Assessor.*

heel of the Pope. But such, on their own showing, are traitors and perjurers. The notion that a loyal churchman, who is in no danger of conversion to Rome, and rejects Rome's claims, should yet be willing to think of a *rapprochement* – this is what baffles and perplexes many a Protestant abroad.'[1]

Here, then, are two opposite poles – Rome saying: 'We are the true Church: come to us', and Protestantism saying: 'We are the Church of the New Testament: have nothing to do with them'.

Heedless of the accusation of being 'traitors and perjurers', the Anglican Church has always felt that, distant and daunting though it may be, the goal of Unity, which must clearly involve the Church of Rome, should not be finally abandoned. This comes out in the reports of successive Lambeth Conferences, where we can detect, under the expressions of despair, a faint hope that one day the walls of partition may be breached and *all* may be *one*.

In 1867 the Lambeth fathers did no more than warn the faithful against 'the growing superstitions and additions with which in these latter days the truth of God hath been overlaid . . . especially by the pretension to universal sovereignty over God's heritage asserted for the See of Rome'. The second Conference in 1878 was even more dispirited, having had to face the declaration of Papal Infallibility by the Vatican Council in 1870. In 1888 the spirit was one not so much of protest as of regret. 'The Committee', they wrote, 'with deep regret felt that, under present conditions, it was useless to consider the question of Reunion with our brethren of the Roman Church, being painfully aware that any proposal of reunion would be entertained by the authorities of that Church only on condition of a complete submission on our part to those claims of absolute authority, and the acceptance of those other errors, both in doctrine and in discipline, against which, in faithfulness to

[1] G. K. A. Bell, *Christian Unity* (London, 1948), p. 58.

God's Holy Word, and to the true principles of His Church, we have been for three centuries bound to protest.'

When the Conference next met, in 1897, the fathers were still smarting from what has been described as 'one of the sharpest and most public rebuffs that the Church of Rome can ever have administered to a peaceful Christian Communion'[1] – the decree *Apostolicae curae* (1896), which concludes with the words: 'We pronounce and declare that ordinations performed according to the Anglican rite have been and are absolutely null and utterly void'. But, in spite of this, the Anglican fathers still nourished some hope. In fact, they thought things were perhaps improving a little, and could even record their thankfulness that a better spirit seemed to be blowing through the corridors of power at Rome.

This spirit of hopefulness had increased considerably by the time the Conference met in 1908, when the fathers rejoiced that Roman Catholic theologians were now beginning to enter the field of modern scholarship and that some of the Protestant Churches were at last beginning 'to look with sympathetic hope towards that great [Roman Catholic] communion as embodying ideals which they find to be largely lacking in much of the sectional Christianity of today'. They, therefore, felt able to make this momentous statement, namely that '*there can be no fulfilment of the Divine Purpose in any scheme of reunion which does not ultimately include the great Latin Church of the West*, with which our history has been so closely associated in the past, and to which we are still bound by many ties of common faith and tradition'. But the initiative lay with her. 'Any advance . . . is at present barred by difficulties which we have not ourselves created, and which we cannot of ourselves remove.'

When the Conference next met, in 1920, the bishops felt a strong desire to do something for Christian Unity. The world had just passed through the terrifying and bewildering experi-

[1] G. K. A. Bell, *op. cit.*, p. 68.

ence of the first Great War. The outbreak of war on such a scale, the sufferings which it had caused, the atrocities which had been committed had all been a great shock to Christian consciences. But, by 1920, everyone liked to believe that such a tragedy could never occur again. It had been the 'war to end wars'; and now, with the creation of the League of Nations, the world was entering on a new era of peace and fellowship. So the Lambeth fathers, meeting within a year of the signing of the Peace Treaty, made 'Fellowship' or 'Comradeship' the basis of their talks. 'One idea', they said, 'runs through all the work of this Conference. . . . It is the idea of fellowship'. A divided world was now drawing together again in fellowship; the time had come for a divided Church to do the same. On the basis of this hope the Conference launched 'An Appeal to All Christian People'.

The Appeal was a brave and imaginative venture which undoubtedly did a great deal to break down some of the barriers of suspicion and distrust which had existed for so long between the Anglican Communion and other reformed Churches. It has, therefore, played its part in the creation of the atmosphere of cordiality and mutual recognition and respect which we enjoy today. The fact that the bishops could declare that they did not 'call in question for a moment the spiritual realities of the ministries of those Communions which do not possess the Episcopate', but that they could 'thankfully acknowledge that these ministries have been manifestly blessed and owned by the Holy Spirit as effective means of grace' was music in the ears of people who were used to being described as 'dissenters', if not something worse. But the appeal inevitably met with a good deal of criticism from the leaders of the Free Churches in England and was virtually ignored by the Roman Catholic and Orthodox Churches.[1]

The heart of the Appeal is a 'vision' of a Church in which all

[1] See the various replies printed by G. K. A. Bell in *Documents on Christian Unity, 1920–24*, (Oxford, 1924), pp. 104–42.

who regard themselves as followers of Christ will find themselves at one in 'an outward, visible and united society, holding
one faith, having its own recognised officers, using God-given
means of grace, and inspiring all its members to the world-wide
service of the Kingdom of God'; but one has only to read the
Appeal through to realise that, although it was addressed to 'all
Christian people', and although copies were sent to the Pope
and the Patriarch of Constantinople, the Anglican fathers were,
in fact, appealing to members of the non-episcopal Churches,
and were thinking, therefore, in terms of Church unions rather
than of Christian unity. The new fellowship which they envisaged could, in fact, be no more than a union of the Anglican
Communion with some of the other Churches of the Reformation. Proposals are made in the Appeal whereby an episcopal
ministry might be conveyed to those who lacked it; but nothing
was said about the recognition of Anglican orders by the
Roman Catholic and Orthodox Churches, or what these large
and influential bodies were likely to think of the 'recognised
officers' of the new, united Church. The language of the Appeal
is moving, but the hopes are illusory. Christendom was not then
– nor is it now after nearly half a century – in a position to sink
its differences, wipe out its past, abandon some of its deepest
convictions and respond with more than courtesy to the vision
of 'a Church, genuinely Catholic, loyal to all Truth, and gathering into its fellowship all "who profess and call themselves
Christians", within whose visible unity all the treasures of faith
and order, bequeathed as a heritage by the past to the present,
shall be possessed in common and made serviceable to the whole
Body of Christ'.

   The Appeal was obviously not going to make any difference
to the relationship between the Anglican Church and the
Church of Rome, which remained as cool as ever. But if the
Church as a whole could not do much, there were interested
individuals anxious to pursue what we should now call 'dia-

logue', with a view to better understanding and possibly to some tentative steps towards recognition. The pioneer in this on the Anglican side was Lord Halifax, whose conversations with Cardinal Mercier at Malines in 1921–23, created a certain amount of interest. There have been conversations with various groups since then; but the wall of partition has remained as impregnable as ever.

The Anglican Church has, therefore, inevitably had to turn all its ecumenical vigour towards schemes and plans for partial unions in various parts of the world. Some believe that such local unions among non-Romans are positive steps towards the final Unity which is our ultimate goal. 'Are not the mending of the schisms of the eighteenth and seventeenth centuries', writes D. M. Paton, 'by the recovery of unity with the Methodist Church, the Church of Scotland, and the other English Free Churches in these islands, and the consummation of the comparable plans for unity in other Anglican Churches our first task? And is not the meaning of these unions *not* that we are "moving in a Protestant direction away from Catholicism" but *rather taking the first step on the way to Orthodoxy and Rome?*'[1] This is a question to which there is no clear answer, but one to which a great deal of thought must obviously be given. There are, however, a good many who feel that Christian Unity is too subtle a thing to be brought about just by a joining together of broken fragments, like an archaeologist gradually piecing together the bits of a Greek vase. As a group of Anglicans wrote in 1947: 'The re-union of Christendom cannot be a fitting-together of broken pieces, but must spring from a vital growth towards a genuine wholeness or catholicity of faith, thought and life.'[2]

Since the Church of Rome was so aloof, Anglican ecumenists

---

[1] D. M. Paton, *Anglicans and Unity* (London, 1962), p. 106. The italics are his.

[2] *Catholicity: a Study of the Conflict of Christian Traditions in the West* (London, edition of 1952), p. 10.

have tended to find their spiritual home in the World Council of Churches which came into existence in 1948. Here was a vigorous, active, well-informed, optimistic body of people who cherished a vision of a great union of all non-Roman Churches and societies, and put all their energies towards achieving it. The World Council of Churches reached its greatest triumph when the Assembly met at New Delhi in 1961, and, like the Anglican fathers in 1920, gave to the world a vision of a united Church 'as all in each place who are baptised into Jesus Christ and confess him as Lord and Saviour are brought by the Holy Spirit into one fully committed fellowship, holding the one apostolic faith, preaching the Gospel, breaking the one bread, joining in common prayer, and having a corporate life reaching out in witness and service to all'.[1] But, also like the Anglican fathers in 1920, this vision was not seriously intended to include the Church of Rome, and again it looked as if the only hope for Christendom lay not in Unity but in Duality as Rome and and non-Rome faced each other across the great divide.

While the representatives of the non-Roman half of the Christian world were meeting in New Delhi, the other half was stirring in its ecumenical sleep in Rome. For, three years previously, a man called Angelo Roncalli had been elected as pope and was already beginning to change the whole face and shape of Christendom. Pope John, as he chose to be known, was an old man. At the time of his election, on 28 October, 1958, he was nearly seventy-seven and, therefore, long past the age at which most men retire from active work. Few people imagined that he would do much during his pontificate. It could not, anyhow, last very long, and old men are expected to 'dream dreams' rather than to 'see visions'.

But Pope John turned out to be much more of a visionary than people expected. Less than three months after his election, on

[1] *New Delhi Speaks* (London, 1962), p. 55.

25 January, 1959, he announced to a startled world that he intended to summon a Council. The idea seemed preposterous. There had been only twenty such Councils in the whole history of the Christian Church, and each one had been called to deal with some particular emergency. The last Council, which had met in 1869, had been thought by many to have brought the series to an end. For, by declaring the dogma of Papal Infallibility, there seemed no need for further Councils. Everything now was in the hands of the Supreme Pontiff, who could call upon such advice as he needed and issue such edicts as he wished. The idea of bringing together the 2,300 bishops and others who would have the right to attend seemed ridiculous; and the members of the Roman Curia, who would be most concerned in the running of the Council, were mystified and apprehensive. John had apparently consulted no one about the need for, or business of, a Council. Was this a sign that the old man was failing? Some of the cardinals thought that they had elected him as a 'caretaker' pope, and it is not the duty of caretakers to change all the furniture round or perhaps even pull down parts of the house! What is sometimes known as 'Piononismo' – the old, intransigent outlook of Pio Nono (Pius IX) – had become well-established in the Vatican. The Curia wielded great power over members of the Church in all parts of the world. There was no real threat either to the power of the Curia or to the prestige of the Papacy. So why hold a Council?

But Pope John stuck to his guns. The call to hold a Council was, he believed, of divine origin and could not, therefore, be disobeyed. Although, to members of the Curia, safely established in their offices in Rome, the Church might seem to be running pretty smoothly, John (who had lived in Bulgaria, Turkey and France) knew something about the troubled state of the world and about the divisions among Christians. He saw the world in imminent danger of self-destruction. He saw a steady drift away from the Christian religion. He saw those

who are called to mutual love quarrelling among themselves.
And he was a warm-hearted and pastorally-minded man. Of
course he was old. Of course he could not expect a long pontificate. But he was not prepared just to potter about the Vatican
in his embroidered slippers, smiling benignly on adoring
pilgrims. If the Holy Ghost had moved the cardinals to elect
him as their leader, they must take the consequences.

So, in spite of the misgivings of those who really did not relish
the idea of a Council at all, the preparations for this vast con-
course were put in hand. First, the bishops had to be asked
what subjects they would like to discuss. Then Commissions had
to be appointed to work their way through the mountain of
material sent in from all parts of the world, and prepare the
draft decrees (Schemata) which the Council would debate.
Then there were the practical problems to be faced, including
the turning of the nave of S. Peter's into a vast debating
chamber. Finally, I suppose there must have been some
financial anxiety, as I was told that the sessions of the Council
cost the Church 1,000 dollars a minute![1] So, for over three years,
a large number of people were kept busy making the necessary
preparations, all made more difficult by the fact that no one
living had ever attended a Council before and so had no personal experience of how it would work. (Old Bishop Carinci,
born in 1861, had been a small boy running about the streets
of Rome in 1869; but he was honest enough to confess that he
had no recollections of Vatican I). So everyone had to start
from scratch, and learn the rules as he went along.

Pope John had from the first made it clear that he wanted
the Council to be concerned with two great issues – Renewal
(which he called *Aggiornamento*) and Reunion (or *Ecumenismo*).
He realised that the two things must go together. He knew that

---

[1] The actual cost to the *Vatican* has been disclosed as £14,217 for each
morning's work – i.e. about $200 a minute. But, of course, the cost to the
Church was much greater than that.

many people outside the Roman obedience were critical of the
Church. He knew, therefore, that, if the Roman Church was
going to make itself look more attractive to those outside it, then
it would have to carry out a number of reforms. Thus, from the
very start, he had said: 'First there must be a Council to reform
the Church and to revive the spirit of the Gospel. Then we
shall be able to understand our separated brethren, and they
will understand us' (25 January, 1959). On Whitsunday, 1960,
he developed this further:

> 'We believe it to have been (he said) at the bidding of God himself
> that the idea came to us, almost immediately after entering upon
> our pontificate, of celebrating an ecumenical Council, like the
> flowering of an unexpected spring. From such a solemn assembly
> of the sacred hierarchy, gathered around the Roman Pontiff, the
> Church, the beloved Bride of Christ, can derive a new and greater
> splendour in these troubled times, and a new hope arises that
> those who rejoice in the name of Christians, but who are neverthe-
> less separated from this apostolic see, hearing the voice of the
> divine Shepherd, may be able to make their way into the one
> Church of Christ.'

In these words John laid down the purpose of the Council –
to give a new and greater splendour to the Church so that those
outside it will be moved to come in. The words sounded
ominous to Christians of other communions. Everyone in the
ecumenical movement was aware of the fact that Christian
Unity was not going to be achieved by one Church absorbing all
the rest. If this was all that the Roman Church had to offer,
then there was not much point in discussing the matter with
them.

And yet . . .? This was, after all, the first time that the Church
of Rome had begun to take much interest in the 'separated
brethren'. Ought we not perhaps (they said) to look a little
more closely at what she is doing? Can it be that God is calling
us now to try to sew up the greatest of all rents in the seamless
robe of Christ?

So it was that, when the Council opened on 11 October, 1962, there stood before the Pope a group of observers, sent by their respective Churches on a mission of goodwill, to watch over the affairs of the Council and to see how far it was promoting the cause of Christian Unity.

CHAPTER TWO

The Observers

ABOUT FORTY MEN FORMED THE GROUP OF OB-
servers who occupied the places of honour in S. Peter's on
the morning of 11 October, 1962, when the Second Vatican
Council was officially opened. We had met in the offices of the
Secretariat for promoting Christian Unity in the Via dei Cor-
ridori at 7.30, and had been taken by the secretaries to the
basilica. The vast church was swarming with people, and we
naturally wondered very much where we should be put and
what likelihood there was that we should be able to observe anything at all. To our surprise and joy we found ourselves being
conducted to a semicircle of chairs, placed in front of the tribunes and close to the *confessio* so that, when the Pope arrived,
we should be occupying the front seats, closer to the Holy
Father than even the most exalted of his own faith.

The group of non-Roman Catholic visitors came from many
different Churches. Two – a priest and a layman – represented
the Coptic Church of Egypt; one the Syrian Orthodox Church;
two were Ethiopians; Fr Sarkissian belonged to the Armenian
Church, and two represented the Russians in exile. Canon
Maan was there on behalf of the Old Catholics; Professor Fred
Grant, Archdeacon de Sousa, Canon Pawley and myself represented the Anglican Communion; and there were Lutherans,

Calvinists, Congregationals, Methodists, a Quaker and a representative of the Disciples of Christ. There were also representatives of the World Council of Churches, two brothers from the Taizé Community (Roger Schutz and Max Thurian), Professor Oscar Cullmann (who has perhaps done more than anyone else to disprove the papal claims) and a Baptist negro from Chicago, who had to be treated as a guest of the Secretariat as his Church had decided not to send delegate observers to the Council.

This group, therefore, represented a very large part of the non-Roman world. But there was one notable omission. There were no representatives of the Orthodox Churches. This was very much regretted, though it was partly remedied by the arrival on the following day of Fr Borovoi and Fr Kotliarof to represent the Church of Russia. Great efforts had been made to see that the Eastern Orthodox Church was represented; but these had failed. The patriarch, Athenagoras I, would dearly have liked to send observers; but some of the Churches under his jurisdiction thought that they would compromise themselves if they became in any way involved in the work of the Council, and refused to play. In the spring of 1963 I was sent on a mission of goodwill to the patriarch in Constantinople and to the Archbishop of Athens; but, whereas the former could only express his regrets, the latter made it quite clear that he thoroughly disapproved of the whole affair. The situation improved slightly, however, by the arrival, in the middle of the First Session, of Bishop Cassien who, though not an official delegate of the Eastern Orthodox Church, was at least in communion with it.

As the years went by, this group of observers grew. In 1963 there were representatives of the Syrian Orthodox Church of India, the Armenian Church of Etchmiadzin, the Mar Thoma Syrian Church of Malabar and the Church of South India; and in 1965 observers came from the Bulgarian Orthodox Church, the United Church of Christ in Japan, and the Australian Council of Churches. There was also an increasing number of Greek and Russian Orthodox – one as a representative of the World Council of Churches, others personally nominated by the patriarch. By the end of the Fourth Session the group had grown to nearly 100. This was partly due to the fact that few people could be there all the time and had to have substitutes to sit in for them when they were away. The result was that a good many people managed to get in, some of them only for a very short time. No doubt they thought it worth their while. To have been an observer at Vatican II carries with it something of a status symbol, and a good many people are, no doubt, going about giving lectures on 'My impressions of the Vatican Council', even though they may have been present for only two or three days. Some of these were among the class of professional ecumenists, who dash around the world in jet planes attending conferences and commissions, and whose livelihood will more or less come to an end in the unlikely event of Christian Unity being achieved before they have reached the age for retirement.

When the Archbishop of Canterbury was invited to nominate three people to represent the Anglican Communion, he decided that, so far as it was possible, one should come from the British Isles, one from the East and one from the American continent. This was important as it emphasised the fact that the Anglican Communion is no longer a national Church, but a world-wide institution. There has always been, therefore, among our observers, one who was non-white – Archdeacon (now Bishop) de Sousa, Bishop Zulu of Transkei, Bishop Cuba'in of Lebanon and Fr Ernest John of the Brotherhood of the Ascension in Delhi. Our transatlantic delegates have been Professors F. C. Grant, W. J. Wolf, Eugene Fairweather and Massey Shepherd – all competent theologians upon whose knowledge we have freely drawn. The other members of the Anglican delegation were Professor Howard Root, Canon Welsh of the College of

Preachers at Washington, Dr Peter Day and Mr John Law-
rence. In addition we have benefited greatly from the presence
of the two personal representatives in Rome of the Archbishop of
Canterbury – Canon Bernard Pawley and Canon John Findlow.

The observers very quickly got to know one another and
became a closely-knit fellowship. We sat together every day in
the observers' tribune in S. Peter's. We shared the same experiences, laughed at the same jokes, followed the work of the
Council together and discussed its personalities. Many of us
lived together at a small hotel, the Castel Sant'Angelo, which
was familiarly known as 'The Observatory'. Twice a week some
of us met and prayed together in the little Methodist Church
just across the Tiber. We were, therefore, thrown very much
together; and attempts were made, from time to time, to try to
weld us into a sort of supra-denominational Church, a non-
Roman amalgam. But these attempts failed. We were, of course,
all 'separated brethren', not in communion with the see of
Rome, but neither were we in communion with each other, and
in fact represented very different traditions – Orthodox, non-
Chalcedonian, Anglican and Protestant. Some of the observers
hoped that we should put up a united front on various matters;
but it was impossible to do so. For example, it was suggested,
early on in the First Session, that during the Daily Mass, with
which each congregation of the Council began, we in the
observers' box should try to show some uniformity – either
stand or sit or kneel. But this was clearly impossible. Russians
and Methodists don't normally kneel, whereas Anglicans and
the Taizé brothers naturally wanted to genuflect at the more
solemn moments in the liturgy. Or again, attempts were made
from time to time to get us to act together by signing mani-
festoes or sending petitions to the Pope or the Secretary General
or the Presidents. All this some of us resisted. Although we
formed a natural group – known in the Council as *acatholici* –
and although our non-Romanism was a very real bond in the

face of such vast numbers of Romans, we knew that we were not a 'Church', and any attempt to behave as if we were would have been certain to fail.

All our work at the Council was done in conjunction with the Secretariat for the Promotion of Christian Unity. The idea of forming such a Secretariat appears to have come from Cardinal Bea who, in March 1960, asked the Pope if he would consider setting up a commission to study the ecumenical aspects of the Council.[1] Bea is a German Jesuit, born in 1881 and a scholar of distinction. He had lectured at the Gregorian University, and for nearly twenty years had been Rector of the Pontifical Biblical Institute. But the most important thing about him was that he had for long been taking an interest in ecumenical matters, and knew a great deal about what was going on in the non-Roman half of Christendom.

Pope John was obviously pleased with the suggestion, and on 30 May, 1960, he announced that he would set up a Secretariat 'to help the Separated Brethren to follow the work of the Council'. A week later he appointed Cardinal Bea as its president. Bea immediately won the confidence of the observers. There is in him no trace of that triumphalism, or arrogant curialism that the Protestant mind so hates and fears. A kindly, affectionate, quiet, simple, elderly and holy man, Cardinal Bea came to be the symbol of the new spirit in the Church of Rome. The observers both loved and admired him. We felt he was on our side, our leader, our particular friend, almost our father-in-God. At all great ceremonies he was the one whom we watched. We knew that we could trust him because he was so obviously a good man; and Dr Douglas Horton pleased us all very much when he reminded us that BEA is half way to BEATUS.

Under Cardinal Bea's leadership the Secretariat gradually came into being. On 24 June, 1960, Fr Willebrands was

[1] R. Kaiser, *Inside the Council* (London, 1963), pp. 33-8.

brought from Holland, where he had taught theology and been
secretary of the Catholic Conference on Ecumenical Questions,
to be its secretary. He was assisted by two sub-secretaries, the
genial and captivating Corsican, Fr Arrighi, and the quiet and
competent French White Father, Fr Duprey. These, together
with Frs Stransky, Long and Salzman, formed the executive of
the Secretariat for Unity.

From the first it was clear that enormous trouble was being
taken to see that we were given every facility to make our work
both profitable and enjoyable. In spite of warnings said to have
been expressed by some of the fathers, we were given copies of
all the confidential documents, sometimes with translations.
In the *aula* of S. Peter's we sat in the tribune of S. Longinus,
close to the Presidents and Moderators and immediately next
to the secretaries. Here we had a splendid view of all that was
happening, and were far more integrated into the proceedings
than were many hundreds of bishops whose seats were so far
away from the centre of things that they could see practically
nothing of what was going on. I used sometimes to stroll down
to the far end of the basilica only to find the junior prelates be-
having rather like fifth-form boys when the master was out of
the room. Some were talking, some reading newspapers, some
writing letters. Poor things! How they must have envied us in
our privileged position! So conspicuous and so privileged were
we that, when the Holy Father visited the *aula*, he always paused
for a moment to greet us as he walked towards the lift which
was to bear him to the lonely isolation of his own apartments.

On all big occasions we always had front seats. When these were
conciliar ceremonies, we generally sat, as on the first morning,
on chairs in front of the tribunes of S. Andrew and S. Longinus.
Here we had a magnificent view of all that went on; and could
be seen as well as being ourselves able to see. For, speaking to
us about the opening service of the Council, Pope John said:
'I confess to you that it was, for me, a day of great emotion. On

that providential and historic occasion I devoted all my attention to my immediate duty of preserving my recollection, of praying and giving thanks to God. But my eye from time to time ranged over the multitude of sons and brothers; and suddenly, as my glance rested upon your group, on each of you personally, I drew a special comfort from your presence. I will not say more about that at the moment, but will content myself with recording the fact. . . . Yet, if you could read my heart, you would perhaps understand more than words can say.'

In our tribune we were provided with interpreters, devoted men who made it possible for us to understand what was going on. Not only did they give us running translations, they also attached themselves to our group in many ways, and were always ready to help us in understanding the manoeuvres and political moves which were constantly being made in the debates.

The rule of the Council was that all speeches must be made in Latin, and the only speaker to break this rule was the Melkite patriarch, Maximos IV, who, after offering to speak in the language spoken by our Lord, lapsed into French. Other speakers obeyed the rule, but many of us found them very difficult to follow. It was assumed that every Roman Catholic bishop would be so versed in the Latin language that he would have little or no difficulty in following what was being said. But many of them were baffled, though Cardinal Cushing of Boston was one of the few who was honest enough to admit that he couldn't make head or tail of it all. 'You know', he once said to me, 'I've never been properly educated. I never was taught Lat'n properly at school. I was at Boston in World War One an' we never learnt any Lat'n there. So I can't understand a word these guys say. I jus' have to look intelligent an' get someone afterwards to tell me what it's all about.'

Pope John – perhaps unfortunately – had, a few months before the Council, issued an apostolic constitution in praise of Latin which he called *Veterum Sapientia* and in which he had

declared that he was 'fully determined to restore this language
to its position of honour and to do all we can to promote its
study and use'. Having said this, he proceeded to take some
Latin lessons in order to set a good example.[1] But many of the
fathers, especially those who had not had the advantage of
several years of study in Rome, found the Latin very difficult.
Many of them would have liked simultaneous translation, and
there were rumours from time to time that a system was about
to be installed. It was even said that Cardinal Cushing had
offered to pay for it (just as, out of the kindness of his heart, he
was said to have offered to have the whole of hell air-condi-
tioned). But no apparatus was installed. There seemed to be
two difficulties – one being the vast equipment necessary to
serve 2,500 people; the other the difficulty of finding competent
translators. For speed and accuracy in such work requires long
training and practice, and, whereas there were plenty of professional translators who could turn French into Russian, or German
into Italian, none of them had ever had to deal with Latin.

So the fathers were left to struggle along as best they could.
But some pity was shown to the observers, none of whom had
had much practice in understanding *spoken* Latin. All of us had
some knowledge of the language, or there would not have been
much point in our being there; and some became quite proficient
in following what was said. But it was never easy, for each
speaker had his own particular accent, and Italian Latin
differed considerably from French, French from American,
American from Japanese, and so on.

In addition to helping us to understand the Council, the
Secretariat for Unity did its utmost to enable us to enjoy it.
There was little time for sightseeing, but arrangements were
made for us to visit the Vatican Library, the excavations under
S. Peter's and some of the churches in Rome. On Saturdays,
when the Council did not sit, more ambitious expeditions were

[1] John XXIII, *Journal of a Soul* (London, 1965), p. 322.

sometimes planned. Places visited included the Benedictine
Abbey at Subiaco where, for the first time in 1,500 years, ladies
sat down to their *colazione* in the monks' refectory; Assisi, where
we were royally and lavishly entertained by the friars in the
Sacro Convento; Castel Gandolfo where, after partaking of
'tea' (which included Asti spumante and white wine) we visited
the papal observatory and listened to clergymen talking to us
about the behaviour of meteorites; Monte Oliveto, Grotta-
ferrata, and other places. Members of the Secretariat generally
accompanied us on these outings which, if exhausting, were
nevertheless very pleasant and instructive. Everywhere we
went we were treated as honoured guests, and generally came
back loaded with presents – pictures, books, bottles of liqueur,
etc. If Christian Unity were no more than a question of prodigal sons returning to their father's house – 'we are inviting
you not to the home of a stranger but to your own, your
Father's house' (Pope John) – many of us would be tempted to
go there tomorrow if the standard of living is anything like
what we saw.

Once a week the observers met with members of the Secretariat for Unity to discuss the subject then being debated in the
aula. These meetings were of great importance. During the
First Session we met in a room in the Hotel Columbus and sat
round a long table, very inadequately lit, to discuss our problems.
With the increase in the number of observers in subsequent
years, we had to move to more spacious quarters, which were
found for us at the Foyer Unitas in the Piazza Navona. The
Foyer Unitas, under the efficient and friendly care of the Ladies
of Bethany, has now become a great ecumenical meeting-place
in Rome. It began many years ago when Fr Charles Boyer, S.J.
made a point of meeting non-Roman visitors and giving them
an opportunity of discussing problems of Christian Unity with
intelligent Roman Catholics. I first discovered this in 1950 when

I visited Rome with a party of students, who were delighted to discover what they called 'Boyer's Foyer'. In those days meetings were held at the Brigittine monastery in the Piazza Farnese, or in a road near the Venerable English College; but recently they have acquired more spacious accommodation. The big room in the Foyer Unitas gave us all that was needed for our weekly meetings.

At these meetings some expert came to speak to us about the Schema then under discussion, and we could then ask questions or give our own opinions on it. The proceedings were conducted normally in English and French, and those who could speak only in Russian or German had to have interpreters. From these discussions we learnt much, both from our guest speakers and from each other; and, if the German Lutherans and Greek Orthodox tended to talk too much, it was partly our fault for not talking enough.

Apart from these Tuesday meetings at the Foyer Unitas, we had boundless opportunity for meeting the Council fathers and discussing things with them. In S. Peter's itself, from about 11 o'clock onwards (the hour at which the coffee-bars opened) there was considerable movement in the side-aisles and transepts, and it was here (and in the bars) that we met so many people and talked about so many things. There were also the news-conferences, the public lectures, the press-conferences, the receptions and dinner-parties, the little groups which formed themselves outside the cafes over a *cappuccino* or *espresso*. Everywhere we went we were picking up information, making new friends, discussing some theological or practical issue. Most of the fathers seemed pleased that we were there. As I wandered about S. Peter's in an obviously Anglican purple cassock, bishops, and even cardinals, would come up and say: 'Are you the Bishop of Ripon?' after which we could get down to conversation on some matters of mutual interest and concern.

In this way the observers gradually became integrated into the life and work of the Council. During the meetings of the

Council the only people allowed inside S. Peter's were the Council fathers, the secretaries, the *periti* and (after the First Session) the auditors. It was, therefore, a 'closed shop' and, though the numbers were large (about 2,500) we came to feel very much united. As soon as the initial suspicion of the observers, and what they were up to, had been overcome, the fathers, for the most part, accepted us as part of the landscape, while some of them treated us as, in a real sense, involved in the work of the Council; some, when starting their speeches with the customary 'Eminentissimi et excellentissimi patres', would add, 'et dilectissimi observatores', or some such phrase.

When so much was given to us it might seem churlish to complain that we were not given more; but there are two things which I somewhat regret, two points where I think some of us could have been of real assistance to the Council in its attempts to carry out necessary reforms. My first regret is that we were never consulted by the Commissions. These were busy behind the scenes preparing the Schemata on which the fathers would have to vote, and which would eventually become conciliar decrees. On some of the subjects under discussion many of us knew far more even than the members of the Commission. For example, the Liturgical Commission had to discuss ways of worship which, though new to members of the Roman Catholic Church, had been familiar to us for 400 years. I am thinking of things like the use of the vernacular, communion in both kinds, the ministry of the Word, and so on. I am sure that, if we had been approached, we should have been able to give valuable help on these matters. In the same way, many of the controversial subjects included in the famous Schema 13 on 'The Church in the Modern World' were matters on which some of the observers were experts of international reputation who would have had much to offer. Similarly, questions such as married clergy, a permanent diaconate, diocesan synods, the ministry of the laity, were all very familiar to us. But, so far as

I know, no observer was ever invited to help the Commissions
when discussing these things, in spite of the great knowledge and
experience which some of them had. This seems to me a pity.
Good though the work of the Council was, I believe it could
have been made even better if the members had been prepared
to take the visitors a little more into their confidence.

My second regret is that, although the observers became, in
the course of four years, so closely integrated into the work of
the Council none of them was invited to address the Council,
even to express our thanks. In the last few weeks of the Fourth
Session, while voting was taking place, there was a good deal of
time to spare. Some of it was filled up by facetious speeches
from the Secretary General, Archbishop Felici, and some by
music provided by local choirs. But the only way in which the
observers were able to express their thanks and good wishes was
in the form of a letter which was read out by Felici. The long
and enthusiastic applause which greeted this letter made me
feel that the fathers would have been quite happy for one of the
observers to get up and personally convey to the Council the
feelings of gratitude which we all felt. It was, therefore, sad that
this was not allowed.

At the end of the First Session, when I went to say good-bye
to Fr Willebrands, he asked me if I was coming back in the
following year. I told him that I very much hoped to do so,
upon which he said: 'I hope that you will. The presence of the
observers here is very important. You have no idea how much
they are influencing the work of the Council.'

On thinking this over, I began to realise that the presence of
the observers was influencing the Council in three ways. The
first was that we were providing some kind of check on what
was being said. Every bishop who has stood up to speak has
known that, in the tribune of S. Longinus, was a group of intelligent and critical people, their pencils and biros poised to

take down what he said and possibly use it in evidence against him and his colleagues on some future occasion. Pope John had said from the very beginning that one of the main objectives of the Council was to reform the Church in such a way that it would appear more attractive to members of the other Christian communions. Members of the Council tended, therefore, to be very sensitive to what the representatives of those other communions were thinking, and did their best to avoid saying anything which was likely to cause offence. If some father forgot himself and said things which were bound to cause a flutter in the observers' tribune, he was sometimes rebuked by some later speaker. Our presence meant that the Council was much more than just a domestic affair, a matter of the Church discussing her own problems. It was much more than that. It was a real turning-point in Church history, a sign of the entry of the Roman Catholic Church into ecumenical discussion, the inauguration of a new era in Church relations, and it was therefore of extreme importance that she should make a good entry and not tread on the corns of those who were watching her with critical eyes.

Secondly: the fact that the observers were there made it possible for the Council fathers to discover what the rest of the Christian world was thinking about the subjects under debate. Often a chance encounter in the coffee-bar, or in some other part of S. Peter's, led to an enquiry into what we thought (and taught) about such matters as Family Planning or Nuclear Warfare, or to a request for information as to how the 'separated brethren' were likely to react to such problems as Collegiality or Religious Liberty. Most of the bishops were anxious that the Council should help the Church of Rome to draw nearer to the other Christian Churches and were, therefore, glad to have the opportunity of talking things over with the accredited representatives of those Churches in the friendly, if somewhat congested, atmosphere of the Bar-Jonah.

B

Thirdly: although the observers were not allowed to speak in the Council, their speeches were sometimes made for them by one or other of the fathers. For example, on 15 October, 1963, at one of the weekly observers' meetings, Professor Skydsgaard, a Lutheran from Copenhagen, criticised the Schema on the Church, pointing out that something indispensable was lacking in it, namely a sense of judgment. He pointed out that in the Old Testament, and in the New, the Church, which is the People of God, is always represented as in need of God's forgiveness. The 'wrath of God', he said, was emphasised over and over again in the Bible. The People of God had sinned and were desperately in need of God's mercy. What was true of past centuries was true also of this. But this sense of man's treachery and God's mercy was wholly lacking in this Schema, which he described as a 'pale document' since so much was left out. Many of us were impressed by this contribution from a learned theologian who is also a man of great holiness of life. Six days later, as I was going into S. Peter's, one of the observers said to me: 'You remember Skydsgaard's speech at the meeting last week?' 'Yes.' 'Well, you're going to hear it again this morning. Cardinal Meyer has heard about it and is going to make the same points.' Which, sure enough, he did.[1] In a similar way some of the things said about the Anglican Communion in the debate on Ecumenism were undoubtedly the result of conversations which some of the Anglican observers had had with members of the Council.

But if the observers were exercising some influence on the Council, one has a right to ask what sort of influence the Council had on us. This is a more difficult thing to assess; but there is no doubt that most of the observers – and certainly those who spent some considerable time at the Council – came away from it all with a very different, and much more favourable, attitude towards the Roman Church than they had before

[1] X. Rynne, *The Second Session* (London, 1964), p. 115.

it all began. This was almost inevitable, for during the four sessions we became deeply involved in the problems which the Council was discussing, thinking about them and talking about them day and night. Of course some came to the Council in a very critical, if not hostile, mood. As one observer remarked rather cynically: 'It is, of course, more pleasant to feel the warmth of fraternal embrace rather than the acrid heat of inquisitorial flames – but the purpose is the same.' Not all felt as critical as this, but Anglicans had been brought up to believe that 'the Church of Rome hath erred' and that 'General Councils . . . may err, and sometimes have erred, even in things pertaining unto God',[1] while Presbyterians are still tied to the belief (even though they may hold it with certain reservations) that 'the Pope of Rome . . . is that Antichrist, that man of sin, and son of perdition that exalteth himself in the Church against Christ and all that is called God'[2]: though anyone who could believe that John XXIII was all that, could, as they say, believe anything.

But even those most critical of the Church of Rome were to some extent mollified – partly by a feeling of sympathy towards a body of men grappling with difficult problems on which they themselves were not required to pass judgment, and partly by admiration for the progressive and humanitarian approach of those who were determined that this Council should really carry out large and extensive reforms. We all found it difficult to live day by day with people who were just as much concerned as we were about the state of the world, and the need for the forces of Christ to be mobilised and strengthened, and not feel more friendly towards them and more anxious to give them our support.

But perhaps the thing which did most to draw us together

[1] Articles XIX and XXI.
[2] See 'Westminster Confession' in H. Bettenson, *Documents of the Christian Church* (Oxford, 1943), p. 348.

was the fact that we worshipped together day by day. Each
morning began with a Mass in S. Peter's at a nave altar close to
the tribune where the observers were placed. In the early days
some of the observers felt that they could not attend this service.
Bred in more protestant ways of worship, they had always
thought the Roman Mass corrupt, unspiritual, and even, perhaps, hypocritical, and they decided that, rather than sit there
and criticise, they had better stop away. Two things, however,
tended to break down this attitude. One was the fact that, after
the passing of the Constitution on the Liturgy, the way in
which Mass was said became much more simple and congre-
gational; the other that, as the critics became more involved in
the work of the Council, some of their inherited suspicions
tended to thaw out. It was interesting to notice the effect of this
daily act of worship on some of the observers. At first they would
sit rigidly on their chairs, determined to give the impression
that they were there to observe, not to worship. But gradually
they began to follow in their books, to stand for the Gospel, to
bow their heads at the Elevation of the Host, and so on. Some
of us, of course, whose ways of worship were not so dissimilar
from those of the Roman Church, felt more at home from the
start, and could, without twinges of conscience, play a full part
in the daily act of worship with as much concentration as the
Council fathers themselves.

Common prayer, or *communicatio in sacris*, has always been
regarded as a distant goal; but, before the Council ended, we
had joined in a great act of worship in which the observers had
been invited to play their part. This was held, at the Pope's
special request, in the Church of S. Paul's-without-the-Walls on
4 December, 1965. In this vast basilica were gathered together
the Holy Father, about fifty of the cardinals, a large number of
bishops, and the whole group of observers, who sat on the
Pope's left as the cardinals sat on his right. Instead of the usual
'Tu es Petrus' to herald the arrival of Pope Paul, we sang

together 'The Lord is my light and my salvation' (Psalm 27),
which was followed by a collect and a period of silent prayer.
Dr Outler, a Methodist from Dallas in Texas, then read a lesson
from the Old Testament, after whch we all stood up and sang,
in English, 'Now thank we all our God', to the familiar German
tune. Fr Michalon, one of the successors of the Abbé Couturier
in France, then read a passage from the Epistle to the Romans
(in French); we sang another psalm (in Latin), and the Arch-
imandrite Maximos of the Greek Orthodox Church read the
Beatitudes (in Greek). The Pope then preached to us (in French)
– a most moving address in which he thanked us for our co-
operation in the work of the Council and told us that our
departure would leave him with a sense of loneliness which he
had not known before the Council.[1] After this, Fr Davis of
Birmingham, and Canon Maan of the Old Catholic Church,
led us in prayer, and we ended by singing the Magnificat.
Nothing of this kind had ever happened before, and by no
means all the Council fathers approved of it. After all, if, for
many years, you have been teaching the faithful that it is sinful
to worship with schismatics, it is a bit disconcerting if the Holy
Father invites you to do this very thing. There were, therefore,
some empty seats in the church on this occasion. On the other
hand, Cardinal Doepfner, Archbishop of Munich, told me
afterwards that he had found this service the most impressive
moment in the whole Council. He certainly looked as if he was
enjoying 'Nun danket alle Gott'.

   This joint service, which was entirely the Pope's own idea,
was followed by an audience for the observers at which we were
able to express our thanks for all that had been done for us; and
the Pope presented each one of us with a bell – an instrument,
he said, which is designed for the purpose of calling people
together.

   During each session there had been a private audience for

   [1] See below, pp. 207–10, for the text of this address.

the observers, the first being held by John XXIII on 13 October, 1962. On arriving at the Vatican, we were led to the hall known as the Consistory where we awaited the arrival of the Pope. John came in attended by the Secretary of State (Cardinal Cicognani), Cardinal Bea and others, and sat on a chair on the same level with us. This was regarded by the experts in protocol as a most significant gesture, an indication that this was a gathering of friends. After walking round and shaking hands with each of us, he addressed us in friendly terms, gave us his blessing and withdrew. Everyone was delighted. The old idea of the Pope as a mighty potentate before whom man was expected to grovel, even to the extent of kneeling down and kissing his toe, had completely disappeared. Instead, we found a kind-hearted, friendly old man, obviously pleased to have us with him at the Council.

By the time we assembled for the Second Session, Pope John was dead, and Pope Paul reigned in his stead. Again we were summoned to a private audience; but this time, instead of our waiting for the Pope in the Consistory, it was he who waited for us, standing at the door of his library and greeting each one of us as we entered. In fact, we found Pope Paul less formal than Pope John; and, when the customary speeches had been made, he wandered about the room distributing little plaques, for all the world like a Sunday School teacher giving out attendance stamps before dismissing his class. This was typical of Pope Paul. His energy and kindness were staggering; and, of course, he had far more conception of the problems of Christian Unity than Pope John ever had.

No one knows who first had the idea of inviting observers to attend the Council. Perhaps it was Cardinal Bea, who knew a good deal about the non-Roman communions, and who saw the advantages of having representatives from them in the debating-hall. Perhaps it was Pope John who had met members of the Orthodox Church in Istanbul and Bulgaria, and of the French reformed Churches in Paris. Perhaps it just came as a natural development once the 'ecumenical' nature of the Council had been proclaimed and the Secretariat for Unity set up.[1] Whatever its origins, it was a bold and imaginative move, which all must now regard as having met with remarkable success. And, when the history of Vatican II comes to be written, due notice must be taken of this group of men from many countries and many different types of Christian faith and order, who played their silent, but no less influential part, in the *aggiornamento* of the Roman Catholic Church.

[1] See R. Kaiser, *Inside the Council*, pp. 41–2.

CHAPTER THREE

1962: *We say 'No'*

THE OPENING SERVICE OF THE COUNCIL WAS THE
longest service which I have ever attended. It began at 8.o and
ended at 1.30. Yet, though something of an endurance test,
it was not boring. This was partly because so many different
things took place during those five and a half hours, and partly
because the occasion was so impressive. No one had ever been
present at a General Council before. Never before had so large
and so representative a body of Churchmen been assembled
together in one building. As the procession marched across the
square, headed by the papal brass band (whose instruments
never seem to achieve the sonority of English brass), one saw
men from all the corners of the earth, coming to their mother
church in order to dedicate themselves to the task of renewal
for which the Council had been summoned. It was a moving
occasion which reached its most poignant moment when a little
old man of eighty-one dismounted from his portable chair and
walked up the length of the great church to the applause of
those who both loved and admired him.

After the entry of the Holy Father, the service began. First
the *Veni Creator:* then preparatory prayers and a simple Mass
celebrated at a nave altar by Tisserant, the Dean of the College
of Cardinals. Then the procession of cardinals, patriarchs and

heads of religious orders to do homage to the Pope who sat on the platform over the tomb of S. Peter, beaming proudly on his children as they came up to assure him personally of their love and loyalty. Then the Profession of Faith said first by the Pope and then by all the bishops together, their hands on their hearts. Then the prayer 'Adsumus', which in time we came to know more or less by heart as it was said every morning at the opening of the day's sitting. Then a Litany: then a long section in Greek for the benefit of the Uniats: then the Pope's address and the ending. It was a long and exhausting experience for all of us, not least for the old man at the centre of it all. But Sir d'Arcy Osborne, who was well over six feet tall and had a seat fairly high up in the diplomatic tribune, told me that at one moment, when the cardinal-deacons and others gathered round the Pope, he saw one of them open one of the stools and produce a cup of coffee and a sandwich which the Pope consumed with obvious relish.

The Pope's sermon was naturally listened to with close attention, not only by the fathers but by the observers also in the hope of getting some idea as to what line the Council was going to take. John was optimistic. He began by attacking what he called 'the prophets of gloom' who were always forecasting disaster and ruin, and who saw little prospect for the future of the Church. He himself was full of hope. The Council was going to do great things. It was not going to discuss the 'deposit of faith'. That had been done many times, and there was no point in going over it all again. What they needed to do was to find ways in which the Faith could be presented to the modern world in an attractive and compelling way. It would not be the task of this Council to condemn others (no anathemas, presumably), but to win them. Here, naturally, he made some reference to the 'separated brethren', to those who were devout Christians and yet not in communion with the see of Rome. The Council must work so as to bring them into 'the fold'.

As we came away from the basilica, some of the observers were obviously disappointed in what the Pope had said. They had hoped for more inspiration, more imagination. They felt the whole thing not quite worthy of the occasion, a lost opportunity. But our friends at the Secretariat thought it a good speech, and we tried to accept their judgment. Looking back on it now that the Council is over, it is easier to see the speech in its historical context. John no doubt knew that the entrenched forces were strong and determined, and realised that it would have been unwise at this stage to set up ideals which would have been beyond the power of the Council to attain. That indeed would have led to much bitterness in the years to come. But the Council had been warned that there were 'prophets of gloom' in their path. It would be up to them to remove them and march forward to the renewal and rejuvenation of the Church.

The first general congregation was held on 13 October at 9 o'clock, when we discovered what the pattern of the daily assembly was to be. By 8.45 the basilica was filling up, bishops were greeting each other, searching for their seats, finding a quiet corner in which to finish saying their morning prayers, even making a quick confession before settling down to the day's business. Then at 9.0 the bell rang and the bishops dived for their seats, as the little procession left the statue of S. Peter and made its way to the nave altar for the morning Mass. When this was over, another procession came up from the far end of the church for the solemn enthronement on the altar of the book containing the Gospels. This remained there whenever the Council was in session (like the mace in the House of Commons), a perpetual reminder that the whole Council was under the aegis of the Holy Scriptures – an important point when commending the work of the Council to evangelical audiences. Tisserant then led the whole congregation in the prayer 'Adsumus', in which we prayed for the guidance and protection of God; Pericles Felici, the general Secretary, ordered those who were not entitled to attend the Council to leave the church; the doors were closed and the work began.

On this first morning the job of the Council was to elect the ten Commissions who would be responsible for producing the draft texts and for revising them in the light of the debate. In order to get the preliminary work done, a number of preparatory commissions had been appointed by the Pope; but, now that the Council had assembled, it was the job of the fathers to elect new Commissions.

Naturally the work of the Commissions was of great importance. It would be their duty to find out the mind of the Council; to listen to what was said and read what was written; to be prepared to revise and emend a draft decree over and over again until it could be presented in a form which the fathers were prepared to accept. In order to do this, it was very important that the Commissions should be fully representative of the Church, not only geographically but also by having representatives of the progressive as well as the more conservative elements in the Church.

Ten Commissions, each of sixteen members, were to be elected, and on that first morning the bishops were called upon to say whom they wished to have. But how could the poor things know who was suitable? Many came from remote dioceses in the heart of Africa or the midst of the Pacific. On their desks was a list of the 2,300 bishops available, and ten sheets of paper on each of which they were expected to write the sixteen names of the people of their choice. They could not consult their friends, who might be sitting far off. They perhaps could not even converse with the men sitting to right and left of them unless they had some common language. The task was impossible. But, realising that this would be so, the organisers of the Council came to their aid, and kindly provided each one with a list of the members of the existing committees. With this in front of him the poor, bewildered bishop need have no worries. All he had to do was to copy out on the voting papers the list of names which were before him. There was really no difficulty at all.

But some of the more experienced prelates saw what was happening. This was nothing else but a ruse to get the old Commissions reappointed without any new blood and without proper representation of the Council's wishes. Without a moment's hesitation, Cardinal Liénart of Lille, one of the twelve presidents, rose to his feet and said that this would not do. The bishops were in no position to elect their Commissions in this way. What they needed was time to meet in their regional groups and consider carefully how these Commissions should be appointed. No sooner had he sat down than his neighbour, Cardinal Frings of Cologne, got up to second this motion, and it immediately became clear that the Council agreed with this proposed course of action. The first general congregation, therefore, broke up after having sat for only twenty minutes, and many of the cardinals were left standing about while frantic messages were sent out to try and find the cars whose drivers had been told that they would not be required until 12.30.

There is no doubt that this move by Liénart and Frings created something of a sensation. From the way in which the whole thing happened, it appeared that the general secretary and his staff were taken completely by surprise. They had, apparently, assumed that the whole thing would go through without any trouble, and they would get the Commissions they wanted. But it was not to be. The northern European bloc, from whom we were going to hear a good deal in the months to come, had made their first move. They had shown that the fathers were determined to make the work of the Council a real debate in which the opinions of all could be heard. Any idea that the work of the Council was going to be controlled from the Holy Office or any other of the curial establishments, and that the bishops would have to do more or less as they were told, had received its first shock. As Liénart was speaking, we, in the observer's box, began to feel that the Council was going to be interesting and important. When the bishops supported Liénart almost to a man, we knew that the Council was determined to be free and independent. The first shots had been fired. The first 'No' had been said.

The elections took the best part of a week. When they were completed, we soon realised how successful the Liénart-Frings policy had been. The newly-appointed Commissions were far stronger, and far more representative, than what had gone before; and our advisers were happy. The Council could now handle its own business without too much interference from the curia.

When this preliminary job had been completed, the Council could settle down to its first big Schema and its first big debate. This was on the Divine Liturgy; and a fairly long document lay before it – forty-five large pages – dealing first with the theological basis of worship, then with the practical side, then in more detail with the Eucharist, other Sacraments and Sacramentals, the Divine Office, the Liturgical Year, Church furnishing, Church music, and Church art. For fifteen days the Council discussed the principles and proposals laid down in this document.

The subject was naturally of interest to the observers, but especially to the Anglicans, since we have a liturgy which, in many ways, is similar to that of the Roman Catholic Church, and have, ourselves, been closely concerned with liturgical reform and liturgical experiment for some time. We were, therefore, much interested to see what Rome was prepared to do to her liturgical forms now that she had the opportunity.

Many of the Council fathers agreed with us that the Roman Mass was badly in need of reform. Perhaps the most serious thing about it was that it had long since ceased to be an act of

worship in which the People of God could meet together and
offer their praise and thanksgiving to God, and had become
so much more a sacrifice offered by the priest on behalf of the
people. Inaudible and unintelligible, the priest had become
more and more separated from his people, with disastrous
results. All this was totally different from Christian worship as
we read about it in the early Church when the Sunday Eucharist was obviously a great occasion to which all the people contributed. Clement, generally regarded as the third Bishop of
Rome, wrote, about A.D. 95, 'unto the high priest his proper
services have been assigned, and to the priests their proper
office is appointed, and upon the levites their proper ministra-
tions are laid. The layman is bound by the layman's ordin-
ances.'[1] The picture here is of a community worshipping
together, each member playing his part according to his place
in that community. And so it continued for some time. But
gradually more and more of the action was taken over by the
celebrant, so that the people, instead of joining in the worship,
tended to become silent spectators, left very often to make their
own devotions since they could neither hear nor understand
what was being done for them. This change, as Fr Hebert
pointed out, 'shifted the centre of gravity of the service to the
Consecration, and produced the new ceremony of the Elevation,
and in time the new practices of Exposition of the Sacrament
and Benediction. It made the laity no longer in the old sense
participants in the mystery, but spectators of a ritual performed in the sanctuary by the clergy and ministers. Thereby
the sacramental principle itself was in large measure lost,
though its external form remained'.[2] By the later Middle Ages,
in England at any rate, lay people normally made their communion only once a year; and in more recent times, a habit has
grown up of people coming to church to receive the Sacrament

[1] J. B. Lighfoot, *The Apostolic Fathers* (London, 1891), p. 74.
[2] G. Hebert, *Liturgy and Society* (London, 1935), p. 82.

from the tabernacle quite apart from any celebration of the Mass.

Anglican reformers, whether of the sixteenth or of the twentieth century, have tried to remedy this. In the first place they have tried to make the Eucharist, so far as possible, a *corporate* affair. The Prayer Book does this by demanding that there shall be no celebration unless there are at least some to communicate with the celebrant. This has not always been observed. In the high days of the Anglo-Catholic movement, Anglican priests tended to imitate Roman customs; but in more recent time the whole conception of *corporate* worship has been more and more emphasised. Instead of the 'early service' to which only a few could come, the custom in many churches is to have a Parish Communion at a convenient hour when all – men, women and children – can attend. This is an attempt to revive the idea of the Christian community worshipping together, and the rôle of the laity is often emphasised by a layman reading the Epistle, lay people bringing up the bread and wine at the Offertory, and even sometimes a layman assisting with the administration of the elements.

The second principle of the Anglican reformers has been that the service should be *understood*. In order to do this, the liturgy was translated into English in the sixteenth century, and into native languages in the mission field in more recent times. This makes dialogue possible between priest and people, so helping the corporate nature of the action. So important is the idea of people taking an active and intelligent part in the service that many are pleading now for the abandonment of the Tudor English, in which our Prayer Book is written, in favour of a more modern and contemporary style. In the cause of intelligibility, the priest is directed, in the Prayer Book, to say things 'distinctly' or 'with a loud voice' or 'turning himself to the people'. In many Anglican churches the Gospel has, for years, been read from the pulpit or from the chancel step with a view to making it audible.

The third principle of Anglican worship is the importance of *edification*. The Prayer Book demands that a sermon shall be preached at every Eucharist, and, although this rubric is not always observed (and indeed would be impossible in churches where the Holy Communion is celebrated daily) there has been, in recent years, a movement towards a greater emphasis upon the ministry of the Word, especially on those occasions when a reasonably large number of people is present. We have, in the Anglican Church, a great record of preaching; and, although in many places the sermon is, and has always been, associated with Mattins and Evensong, an attempt is being made to ensure that, at the Eucharist, instruction and exhortation are given to the people.

The fourth principle on which Anglican worship is based is one of *obedience* to Christ's commands to 'do this in remembrance of me'. Remembering this, and also his words: 'Unless you eat the flesh of the Son of Man, and drink his blood, you have no life in you' (*John* 6:53), all the reformed Churches have gone back to the primitive practice and given the communion to the people in both kinds, bread and wine. That this was the custom in the early Church, and down to the twelfth century, is not disputed by historians; but, from the time of the declaration of the doctrine of Transubstantiation (in 1215), the chalice came to be more and more withheld from the laity, and, before long, communion in both kinds had become practically unknown in the Roman Catholic Church. To those of us outside that communion, this seemed a surprising, and entirely reprehensible, habit. Nor were we at all convinced by the argument of 'concomitance', which declares that the Body and Blood of Christ are wholly present in either species of the sacrament, which seemed a poor excuse for what would appear to be a total ignoring of Christ's plain words.

We, therefore, read our Schema with considerable interest, wondering how far it would be prepared to go along the path which our reformers had already trodden four centuries ago. We entirely approved of the opening sentence which stated: 'This sacred Council, desiring to augment the Christian life among the faithful day by day, to adapt those ecclesiastical institutions in so far as they have become unsatisfactory (*obnoxiae*) through various changes, to foster whatever may lead to a union in the Church of the separated brethren, and to strengthen whatever is likely to call all men into the bosom of the Church, sees the necessity of reforming and promoting the Liturgy.' Further, we noted the various passages which implied that the Eucharist should become a corporate action in which all could participate, rejoiced that there was a clear recognition that parts of the service should be said in the language of the people, were glad that emphasis was laid on greater use of the Scripture and on preaching, and took note that the principle of communion in both kinds was recognised, even if the practice was to be limited to a few very special occasions such as a wedding or an ordination.

In the debate, which lasted from 22 October to 13 November, a great deal of time was taken up discussing the advantages and disadvantages of the vernacular. The more progressive fathers were all in favour of much greater use of the local languages. Maximos IV pointed out that it was in Aramaic that Christ had offered the first Eucharist, the language of those who shared the experience with him. 'The apostles and the disciples', he said, 'did the same. It would never have occurred to them that, in a Christian assembly, the celebrant should deliver the scriptural lessons, or sing the psalms, or preach, or break bread, in a language other than that of the gathered faithful'. He also went on to point out that, up to the third century, the Roman Church used Greek in her liturgy, but changed then to Latin since that had become the language of the faithful.[1] But the more conservative wing put up a great plea for keeping

[1] X. Rynne, *Letters from Vatican City* (London, 1963), p. 103.

Latin, and Latin only, in the Mass – it was the language of the
Church, Pope John had just commended it to them, it meant
that you got the same service wherever you went, the laity
prefer it as it is, and if you once start translating you can so
easily distort the meaning of the words. As the Italians say:
'traduttore traditore' – a translator is always a traitor. As the
debate progressed, it became pretty clear that there was strong
opposition to the unrestricted use of the vernacular, though it
looked as if the Council would agree to certain parts of the
liturgy being translated. The question also arose as to what
language should be used for the Breviary, the daily offices of
clergy and others. Cardinal Cushing said to me one day (it must
have been fairly early on in the debate, for he left for Boston
after enduring the speeches for a few days), 'It's the Breviary
that they ought to put into the vernacular'. Then, with a sharp
dig in the ribs, 'A man prays best in the language he learnt at
his mother's knee'.

The question as to whether or not it should be made lawful
to administer the Chalice to the laity also came up for debate,
and several influential speakers, including Cardinals Léger,
Alfrink, Lercaro and König, were in favour of it. But there was
much opposition from the conservative wing – Ruffini, Spell-
mann, Michael Browne and others. Cardinal Godfrey spoke
against the idea as he thought that, in England at any rate, it
would look as if the Catholic Church was giving in to the
Anglicans, though many of us thought it might be quite a good
thing if the Catholic Church were to give in, on this point,
to our Lord. Ottaviani made a long speech on the subject –
too long, in fact, as Alfrink had to call him to order after he had
gone on for well over the ten-minute rule, and told him to sit
down. Ottaviani was obviously annoyed by this – no Italian
likes to make what they would call a 'brutta figura' or, as we
should say, 'a fool of himself' – and absented himself from the
Council for the next few days. The poor man probably had a

sore throat, or 'Roman tummy', or something; but the Council
– to whom Ottaviani had become something of a figure of fun –
were sure that he was sulking. It was on this occasion that the
story went round that the reason why Ottaviani was not
present was that he had got into a taxi and, when asked where
he wanted to go to, had inadvertently said 'Trent'.

I discussed this question of communion in both kinds with a
number of bishops. Some of them, while agreeing that it would
be more in accordance with the practice of the Early Church,
said that it was totally impossible to carry out today as it would
take so long. They described the vast congregations in their
churches and assured me that to start communicating people in
both species would enormously lengthen the service. This, however, I showed to be untrue. Every morning the Council began
with a Mass, normally of the Roman rite. But on certain occasions we were able to see one of the Eastern rites as used by the
Uniat Churches. At these quite a number of people communicated, and always in both kinds. The usual system was for the
celebrant to stand holding the Chalice in his left hand. On his
right stood another priest or deacon holding a ciborium, from
which the celebrant took a wafer, dipped it in the wine, and
placed it in the mouth of the communicants as they came up
one by one and stood before him. This simple method did, in
fact, take *less* time than the priest walking up and down the row
delivering the Host. But, when I pointed this out, all they said
was: 'Ah, but we have such enormous numbers of people to deal
with.' So I didn't succeed in making much impression. The
fact that Christ had told us very clearly what he wished us to do
did not seem to 'register' with them at all.

The debate on the liturgy ended on 13 November when the
Schema was handed back to the Liturgy Commission to try
to alter it so as to bring it into line with the views of the Council.
It finally came back during the next session, was voted upon
and finally promulgated on 4 December, 1963. In its final form

it contains much that is good. Look, for example, at the following statements:

> 'It is the duty of the clergy to ensure that the faithful take part
> fully aware of what they are doing, actively engaged in the rite
> and enriched by its effects.' (§ 11.)
>
> 'The Christian people, so far as is possible, should be enabled to
> understand [the services] with ease and to take part in them fully,
> actively, and as becomes a community.' (§ 21.)
>
> 'Rites should be distinguished by a noble simplicity; they should
> be short, clear, and unencumbered by any useless repetitions; they
> should be within the people's powers of comprehension.' (§ 34.)
>
> 'In sacred celebrations there is to be more reading from holy
> scripture, and it is to be more varied and suitable, [and] the
> ministry of preaching is to be fulfilled faithfully and correctly.'
> (§ 35.)
>
> 'The Church earnestly desires that Christ's followers, when
> present at this mystery of the faith [i.e. the Eucharist] should not
> be there as strangers or silent spectators; on the contrary, through
> an adequate understanding of the rites and prayers they should
> take part in the sacred action, conscious of what they are doing,
> with devotion and full collaboration.' (§ 48.)

Then, on the practical issues, the constitution declares that 'the rite of the Mass must be revised . . . and simplified' (§ 50); there must be more use of the Bible (§ 51); a sermon must form part of the liturgy itself (§ 52); a 'Prayer for the Church' or 'Community Prayer' must be restored (§ 53); the vernacular is to be used in certain parts of the service (§ 54); and 'communion under both species may be granted, when the bishops think fit, not only to clerics and religious, but also to the laity' (§ 55).

In all this the Anglican observers were naturally much interested, as it brought the worship of the Roman Catholic Church so much closer to what we are accustomed to. The whole thing reminded me of a notable figure in English musical life some years ago – Arnold Dolmetsch. Dolmetsch was a musician with a great knowledge of, and great love for, the music of the sixteenth and seventeenth centuries. He greatly disapproved of the pianoforte, which he regarded as a coarse modern invention, and devoted his time to making virginals, clavichords and harpsichords, upon which his beloved music could be played. But he was always trying to improve on his instruments, with the result that people used to say that if he went on improving the harpsichord long enough he would one day triumphantly invent the pianoforte. In reading the Schema on the Liturgy, and in listening to the debate on it, I could not help thinking that, if the Church of Rome went on improving the Missal and Breviary long enough, they would one day triumphantly invent the Book of Common Prayer.

It is now more than two years since the Constitution on the Liturgy was promulgated, and we are beginning to see the results. It was not until 1965 that any changes appeared in the morning worship of the Council fathers, but in this, the final session, attempts were made to make the Mass far more a corporate act of worship. We were all provided with books from which we sang psalms for the Introit, Gradual, Offertory and Communion. The Epistle was now read from the pulpit, and the Gospel from a lectern. We also had a short litany or 'Prayer of the Faithful' corresponding to our 'Prayer for the whole state of Christ's Church'. For the psalms, we sang the verses antiphonally with a small, robed choir of men, and we all joined in the Gloria, Creed and Sanctus. Everything was done with great dignity, but we missed the lovely polyphonic music which we used to have in previous years. Incidentally, the new form of service took considerably longer than the old one; so speed cannot be regarded as the most important thing.

As a demonstration of the 'new look' in Roman Catholic worship, a group of young American Jesuits conducted a service each evening at the Jesuit curia in Rome. This I attended one evening, and was amazed to find how different it was from the sort of thing which one had attended so often in Roman Catholic Churches. Six priests concelebrated, facing the con-

gregation across a plain table with two candles on it. We began
with a hymn (sung without accompaniment), and the first part
of the service was all said in English. The Epistle was read by a
layman out of the congregation, and was followed by a period
of silent prayer. After the Gospel, we had a short and simple
address – perhaps rather more personal than didactic – and
then some intercessions in which members of the congregation
were invited to take part by suggesting subjects for prayer.
Then came the Sursum Corda, after which the celebrants lapsed
into Latin for the canon of the Mass, some of which was said
together and some by individual celebrants. After the Kiss of
Peace, in which we all took part, most of the congregation went
up to make their communion, which they did standing. We
ended with another rousing hymn.

All this was very interesting, and I was assured that further
changes would be made, especially that the canon would
eventually be said in English like the rest of the service. But I
must confess that I came away feeling a certain nostalgia for
the dignity and sense of mystery which we try to achieve in our
Anglican services.

The debate on the Liturgy marks the second great 'No' in the
first session of the Council. The traditionalists put up a strong
plea that the fathers should leave things as they were. The
Liturgy had served the People of God for many centuries. Why
change it? Why mess it up in this way? It was the responsibility
of the Congregation of Rites to decide what was best. They
were the experts. They were the men who knew.

But bishops had not come from India and Africa, from the
islands of the Pacific or the West Indies, to be told that a little
group of old men in Rome could tell them what was best for
their flocks. So, once again, they said 'No', and 'authority' had
to bow to their decision.

If some of the more protestant observers got a bit bored by

the long debate on the Liturgy, they woke up when the Council turned from that to consider the next document, which was called 'The sources of revelation'. The moment they opened their copy of the Schema their worst fears were aroused, for the first chapter was headed *'De duplici fonte Revelationis'* – 'on the double source of revelation'. This 'double source' was, of course, made up of the Bible and Tradition, which were to be regarded as of equal authority for the doctrine and teaching of the Church. 'Tradition,' said the text, 'preserved in the Church in continuous succession by the Holy Spirit, contains all those matters of faith and morals which the Apostles received either from the lips of Christ or at the suggestion of the Holy Spirit, and which they passed on as it were from hand to hand so that they might be transmitted by the teaching of the Church.'

This was really going back to the Council of Trent which had put the Bible and Tradition on the same level. In the Fourth Session (8 April, 1546), they had declared that revelation of the truth comes both by written books and by unwritten traditions, received by the Apostles from the lips of Christ or handed down by them at the dictation of the Holy Spirit. These two sources, they said, were to be 'accepted and venerated with equal piety and reverence'.[1] This statement had been more or less repeated at the First Vatican Council in 1870.[2] But it had always been a sore point with the reformed Churches. The *Sola fide* of Luther had been, with many of them, superseded by the *Sola scriptura* of Calvin, and most 'reformation' documents show traces of this. The Anglican 'Articles of Religion', for example, state that 'Holy Scripture containeth all things necessary to salvation, so that whatsoever is not read therein, nor may be proved thereby, is not to be required of any man that it should be believed as an article of faith, or be thought requisite or necessary to salvation' (Art. VI), and every ordination candidate is required to give an

[1] *Conciliorum Oecumenicorum Decreta* (Herder ed. 1962), p. 639.
[2] *Ibid.*, p. 782.

affirmative answer to the question: 'Are you persuaded that the
Holy Scriptures contain sufficiently all doctrine required of
necessity for eternal salvation through faith in Jesus Christ?'
For all this the Anglican reformers could claim considerable
support from the Fathers, for Athanasius had written: 'The
holy and divinely-inspired Scriptures are of themselves sufficient
to the enunciation of truth' (*Contra Gentes*, i), while Augustine
had said: 'In those things which are plainly laid down in Scripture, all things are found which embrace faith and morals' (*De
doctrina christiana*, ii). What, then, is all this about Tradition as
an extra, and equally authoritative, source of truth?

Of course, the question is not quite as easy as it looks. There
must be traditions in the life of the Church which have been
handed down from generation to generation. To begin with, a
whole generation of Christians had grown up before any part
of the New Testament was written at all, so that quite a number
of things had become more or less established before there was
any written word. In a sense it can be said that the Bible is part
of the Tradition, for it was the Church which wrote the Bible
and decided which writings should be included in it.

But the difficulty is that, whereas the Bible is open to all,
Tradition is a kind of secret source of information the true
nature of which has never been revealed. Are we, in fact, to
believe that the Roman Church has access to a separate supply
of divine truth which is not accessible to other Christians? If so,
then any discussion becomes impossible, just as it is impossible
to argue certain things with a Cabinet Minister who has access
to all kinds of secret documents not available to the general
public.

The opening chapter of the Schema on the Bible and Tradition was, therefore, a considerable shock to many of the observers. Here was the Church of Rome turning out the old
stuff, repeating what had been said at Trent and Vatican I,
setting itself up as beyond criticism or argument, claiming to

have received, from Christ himself, its own deposit of truth which no one could discuss as none but Roman Catholics could know what it was. How, they asked, could one have any sort of dialogue with people like this? Did they really suppose that this was the way to attract prodigal sons into their father's house?

But there was more to come. Having dealt with the two sources of revelation, the Schema went on to deal with the inspiration and inerrancy of the Scriptures. 'Since God himself', it said, 'is, by the inspiration (*afflatus*) of his own Holy Spirit the author of the whole Holy Scripture, and, as it were, the writer of it all . . . it follows that each and all the parts of the holy books, even the smallest, must be inspired. . . . It also follows of necessity that the whole of Holy Scripture must be free from all error.' All this was largely based on the encyclical *Providentissimus Deus*, issued by Leo XIII in 1893. It was in criticism of this decree, and of the attitude towards truth which it adopts, that William Temple wrote:

> 'This traditional doctrine of revelation implies that God has so far overridden and superseded the normal human faculties of those through whom the revelation was given as to save their utterances, by voice or pen, from all error in its communication. . . . If Amos and Isaiah and the unknown author or authors of the Books of Kings wrote (as Leo XIII phrased it) "at the dictation of the Holy Ghost" in any sense of those words which could at all justify the use of them – for what "dictation" means in this context is by no means obvious – then no doubt their content must be regarded as truth; but it is truth conveyed in a manner wholly without either parallel or analogy in the normal relationship between God and man, and even contradictory of that relationship.'[1]

Yet in spite of this, and of countless similar statements put out by theologians during the last sixty years, the Theological Commission had cheerfully prepared a document which apparently took no account whatever of what was happening in the world of biblical scholarship.

[1] W. Temple, *Nature, Man and God* (London, 1934), pp. 307–09.

But let us go on. In § 19 the Schema declared, without hesitation, that the Church has always held, and still holds, that the authors of the four Gospels were Matthew, Mark, Luke and John. And in § 25, in praising the Vulgate, it stated that in matters of faith and morals this version is immune from error of any kind and can be quoted without any danger of mistake. And this in spite of the fact that everyone (with the possible exception of the members of the Theological Commission) knew that the Vulgate was an inaccurate translation of a poor text of the Scriptures.

Many of the observers were appalled when they read all this. The document revealed an attitude of mind which was totally out of touch with that of modern scholarship. As one of the observers said to me: 'If they pass this, they will make themselves the laughing-stock of the academic world.' And when you think who were sitting in the *aula* while this document was being presented – Professor Cullmann of Basle and Paris, Professor Maan of Amersfoort, Professor Grant of Union Theological Seminary in New York, Professor Skydsgaard of Copenhagen, Professor Schlink of Heidelburg, Professor Horton of Harvard, and Professor Outler of Dallas – you will realise that there was a considerable section of the academic world there to raise the first laugh.

It was Ottaviani who had to present this Schema to the Council. He knew that many of the fathers were dissatisfied with it, and that various alternative Schemata had been drafted; but he implored the Council to forget about them and accept what the Commission proposed. It was, he claimed, a very good Commission, composed of good scholars who knew what they were doing. But a good many of the fathers thought otherwise.

As soon as Ottaviani had finished, the two dam-busters, Liénart and Frings, started to demolish the case which had been presented. Both pointed out how utterly inadequate the Schema was, hopelessly out of date and calculated to irritate the world

of scholars of all denominations. 'What is said here of inspiration
and inerrancy', said Cardinal Frings, 'is at once offensive to
our separated brethren in Christ and harmful to the proper
liberty required in any scientific procedure.'[1] Ruffini put up a
rather feeble defence of the document, but was immediately
shot down by Léger, König, Alfrink and Suenens, most of
whom thought that the only course was to scrap this text and
write a new one.

With such an array of critics it very soon became clear that
this Schema was not going to get very far. Most of the fathers
realised how ill-prepared it was, and there were several dark
hints about the way in which the Commission had set about its
work, brow-beating opponents of the party line, threatening
them with reprisals if they caused any trouble, and taking
important votes at meetings which the critics could not attend.[2]

Born and bred in such an atmosphere, the Schema was
doomed to failure from the start, and it took only six days to kill
it. Bishops from all over the world got up and attacked it, some
on the grounds that it would make the Church look ridiculous
in the eyes of the world, some that it would widen the breach
between the Roman Catholic Church and the rest of Christendom. It was, perhaps, the second of these which, in the end,
carried the greatest weight, for the *coup de grâce* was really given
by Bishop de Smedt of Bruges, speaking on behalf of the Secretariat for Unity. He showed, from the start, that he wanted to
approach this problem from an ecumenical point of view. He
pointed out the importance of complete honesty and mutual
charity. He laid down certain rules which must be observed if
any profitable dialogue was to take place. He then went on to
reveal that an offer from the Secretariat for Unity to help the
Theological Commission in the preparation of this document

[1] X. Rynne, *Letters from Vatican City*, p. 144.
[2] *Ibid.*, p. 157. First-hand evidence of this was given to the observers by a
distinguished consultant of the Theological Commission.

had been flatly turned down, as had also a proposal for a mixed
sub-commission to look at the whole thing from the ecumenical
standpoint. Many of the bishops agreed with him when he said
that this would not do.

In the judgment of the Secretariat for Unity, the Schema
before them had 'grave faults from an ecumenical point of view.
It would not encourage a dialogue with non-Catholics, or
represent progress, but a retreat. . . . Today, a new method
has been discovered, thanks to which a precious dialogue has
been begun. The fruits of this method are apparent to all in the
presence of observer-delegates in this council hall. The hour is
one of pardon, but also one of great seriousness. If the Schema
prepared by the Theological Commission is not modified, we
shall be responsible for causing Vatican II to destroy a great,
an immense hope. I speak of the hope of those who, like Pope
John XXIII, are waiting in prayer and fasting for an important and significant step finally to be made in the direction
of fraternal unity, the unity of those for whom Christ our Lord
offered this prayer: *ut unum sint*'.[1]

This speech was received with immense applause. It was as if
the bishop had burst into the stuffy office in which the Commission was sitting, had thrown open the windows and said: 'For
God's sake let us have some fresh air in this place.' It was, perhaps, the most important speech of the whole Council. Its
sincerity reduced many of the bishops to tears. It was certainly
the death-blow to *De Fontibus Revelationis*.

So great had been the opposition to the Schema that it had
become impossible to see how the debate could be continued.
After de Smedt's great speech, I noted that the presidents were
holding a meeting after the fathers had gone home to lunch, no
doubt to decide what to do. On the following day we discovered
what they had decided, which was to ask the fathers whether
they felt that this Schema could go on as a basis for discussion.

[1] *Ibid.*, pp. 161–3.

For anything to pass the Council it must have a two-thirds majority. As there were 2,209 fathers present that morning, it would need 1,472 votes to secure such a majority. So Felici, the Secretary General, put the motion in the form: 'Do you wish to throw out this document and try to get another?' When the votes were counted it was announced that 1,368 had voted 'Yes' and 822 'No'. But 1,368 was not a two-thirds majority: so the motion was lost. Had it been put the other way round – 'Do you wish to continue this discussion?' it would, of course, have been heavily defeated. But, having put the vote in this way, there was nothing for it but to continue the debate. Many of the fathers were greatly annoyed about all this. Some thought they had been tricked, and a few may well have voted the wrong way. (As Dr Grant said to me: 'What it means is, if you like this Schema vote *non placet*.') The whole thing certainly left a rather bad taste in the mouth, especially after the hints of tyranny on the part of members of the Theological Commission.

But the next morning the tables were well and truly turned, when a message came down from the Pope that, in spite of the vote, it was clear that the majority of the fathers were dissatisfied with the present Schema. It would, therefore, be withdrawn and a new joint commission, with Cardinals Ottaviani and Bea as joint presidents, would be set up to prepare a new one. The Pope thus did the democratic thing, though in the most undemocratic way.

The wise and courageous action of Pope John saved the situation. The Schema disappeared, and we saw nothing more of it for nearly two years. When it did come back to us it had been completely rewritten, all the offensive parts had been removed, and it passed quietly through the assembly with little comment.

So once again the cry had gone up, 'We say "No".' These bishops were determined to break free from the shackles of the Holy Office and set the Church on the road to *Aggiornamento* and

Ecumenismo. The draft Schema on the two sources of Revelation
would have been a disaster had it been passed in anything
like the form in which it was presented – a disaster for the
movement towards reform and renewal, and a disaster for the
cause of Christian Unity.

Having spent a peaceful day or two on the subject of the
radio, the press, television and suchlike things, it was to the
question of Christian Unity that the Council now turned. The
document before them was called 'On the Unity of the Church:
that all may be one'; but it soon appeared that it was not about
Christian Unity nor concerned that all should be one. It was, in
fact, no more than a draft, drawn up not by the Secretariat for
Unity, but by the preparatory commission set up to deal with
the Oriental Churches with a view to defining the relations
between the Uniat Churches, which are in communion with
Rome, and the Orthodox and non-Chalcedonian Churches,
which are not. In spite of its title, this Schema had nothing to
do with the non-Roman Churches of the West, and was therefore only partially interested in the problem of Unity. Naturally,
a good many of the observers were puzzled by this. They expected that a document which concerned the 'unity of the
Church' would take some notice of the Churches which they
represented; but this was not so. When we asked why this
Schema was so limited, and why it was drawn up quite inde-
pendently of the Secretariat for Unity, we were told that the
Commission disapproved of the Secretariat and had refused to
work in conjunction with them.[1]

Incomplete though it was, this was the first document on
Christian unity to be issued, and the observers fell upon it with
avidity. They were immediately disappointed, not only by its
limitations, but also because of the tone which it assumed and
of the things which it said. Starting from the assumption that

[1] Cf. X. Rynne, *Letters from Vatican City*, p. 191.

the only true Church is that which is in communion with Rome, its only solution of the problem of the divided Churches in the East was to invite the Oriental Churches to follow the example of the Uniats, and accept the authority of Rome. This solution was obviously far too facile, not only for the observers, but for the Council as a whole.

Reading through the Schema the observers soon started putting question marks in the broad margins of the printed text. In § 7 they were told that the unity of the Church cannot be achieved without 'submission' to the authority which Christ instituted, i.e the Papacy. In § 9 they read that, although bona fide members of the separated Churches are not entirely alienated from the true Church, they are deprived of many of the means of salvation. In § 11 they were surprised to hear that 'the Catholic Church has never ceased to work for union', when many of them felt that she had only just begun. And then in § 38 they met the familiar howler (due to one of the mistranslations of S. Jerome in the Vulgate) declaring that Christ had said that there should be one 'fold' and one shepherd, whereas in fact he said one 'flock'.[1]

But it was in the Council itself that the Schema received its roughest treatment. Liénart again led the opposition, saying that all this talk about the Eastern Churches 'returning to the true fold' was ridiculous. Many of them regarded their Churches as older than the Church of Rome, so that, if anyone had wandered away and needed to be recalled, it was the Romans rather than they. It was also absurd to try to attach the blame for Christian division to any one side. All had sinned and all were responsible. But this did not please the conservative Ruffini, Archbishop of Palermo. To him there was no problem at all. The Roman Catholic Church was 'without spot or

[1] The Greek word used in *John:* 10, 16 – *poimné* – means a 'flock', but the Vulgate translates it as *ovile* which means a 'sheepfold'. The Greek for 'fold' is *aulé*, and is used in the same verse.

wrinkle' in its possession of the truth, so that the way to unity was obvious. But this phrase about the immaculate nature of the Church, which is used by S. Paul in a purely eschatological sense, did not pass unnoticed in the observers' 'box', where there were a good many people who knew more about biblical eschatology than Cardinal Ruffini, or indeed than most of the Council.

In the debate it was the Uniats who talked the most sense. These were men who lived side by side with the members of the eastern Churches – Orthodox, Armenian, Coptic, Syrian – and knew something about them. They knew how ancient these Churches were, what great saints and doctors they had known, what splendid liturgies they possessed, what holy lives many of them led. The Roman Church had no right to be condescending or patronising to the Church of S. Basil, S. Cyril, and S. Chrysostom, or to regard its members as in some way second-class Christians. Meanwhile, there were also some western bishops who saw how unsatisfactory this Schema was – men like Bishop Ancel of Lyon, who reminded the Council that it was not for them to condemn those who have gone wrong, especially since Catholics 'have frequently, to say the least, occasioned misunderstandings and difficulties', and Bishop Dwyer of Leeds, who, after criticising the Schema for not understanding the mind of the orientals, told the Council that, unless it showed more charity, it would make a very poor impression on the world.

The debate lasted three days; but it soon became clear that this Schema, as offered to the fathers by the Commission on the Oriental Churches, had little to do with either Christian Unity or Christian Charity; and, when a vote was taken as to whether they should proceed with this document, only thirty-six fathers could be found to support it.

So, once again, the Council said 'No', and said it clearly and firmly.

By the time they had got rid of the so-called Schema on

Christian Unity, the fathers had only six days in which to tackle the Schema on the Church. This was perhaps the biggest subject with which the Council would have to deal, and it was obvious that it could not hope to get very far on a highly controversial document of ninety pages dealing with 'the Nature of the Church Militant', 'Episcopacy', 'the Laity', 'the Magisterium of the Church', 'Authority and Obedience', 'Church and State', 'Ecumenism' and several other subjects. To do this adequately would take several weeks. All that could be done now was to open up the subject and let some of the fathers say what they thought about it. The great debate would clearly now have to be left until next year.

But in the short time available it soon became clear that the Council as a whole was once more critical of what the Theological Commission had provided for it. The document before them reeked of the Holy Office. Among other things it declared:

(1) that there is only one true Church of Christ, the Church Catholic and Roman, which alone is his Mystical Body;

(2) that although all baptised persons have real links with the Church, only those are properly called members who profess the catholic faith, acknowledge the Church's authority, and remain in visible communion with the Pope;

(3) that those who seek to obey Christ must come to the One Church, united in Faith, Communion and Government with the Vicar of Christ;

(4) that not all active participation by dissident Christians in catholic liturgy, or vice versa, can be called intrinsically evil – a point which the observers who attended the daily Mass duly noted – but that there are usually grave reasons for forbidding it;

(5) that catholics may not participate in services of worship with separated communities;

and so forth.

All this sort of thing irritated not only the observers but all the more progressive members of the Council. Over and over again speakers condemned the Schema for being too juridical,

c

too triumphal, too clerical, too legalist, and calculated to offend the 'separated brethren'. Once again we had persuasive speeches from those who had done so much to lead the opposition – Liénart, König, de Smedt, Léger, Doepfner, Suenens, Maximos IV; but perhaps the most interesting speech – not so much for what it said but from the point of view of the speaker – was that made by John Baptist Montini, the Archbishop of Milan. One of the first things I did in Rome was to attend a lecture by Montini on 'Rome and the Council', delivered in the Capitol on the evening of 10 October, just before the Council opened. I was naturally interested in this man, for in 1956 he had invited six Anglicans to go to Milan as his guests for a week in order to talk to him and to some of his people about Christian Unity. I had been one of those invited to go, but had been prevented from doing so at the last minute by the rather sudden death of my mother. Even so, I felt that I knew Montini, and I had in my study a signed photograph which he had sent me. During the first session of the Council he said very little. But he listened intently to all that was said. We observers sat right opposite to the cardinals, and I watched Montini, wondering why he spoke so little. When he did at last get up to speak on this Schema on the Church he immediately showed a real concern for the ecumenical implications of it. Like so many others, he thought this document totally inadequate and wanted it to be completely revised, not by the Theological Commission alone, but in co-operation with the Secretariat for Unity. This speech was well received in the observers' box. It made us feel that this shy, quiet, thoughtful, intelligent little man was quite definitely 'on our side'.

This Schema on the Church, like those which had gone before it, did not get very far. Those who were determined that this Council should really reform the Church soon tore it to bits, virtually telling the Commission that their work was no good and that they would have to start again.

'The Council', said Carli, the garrulous and obstructive Bishop of Segni, 'is slowly petering out before a series of taboos.'[1] And he was right. The First Session was, in fact, a series of refusals, as, one after another, the Schemata, so carefully prepared by the preparatory commissions, were thrown out. Just as the Council had said 'No' when they were expected to re-elect the curially-appointed commissions, so they had said 'No' over and over again when presented with old-fashioned stuff, totally out of keeping with the modern world and, indeed, with the ideals laid down by Pope John. The members of the Council had come from the four corners of the earth. They knew something of the problems with which the Christian Church is faced in countries where life is very different from what you find if you happen to be one of the 5,000 clergymen who work in Vatican city. They knew instinctively that this was a time for action, that the size and importance of the Council gave them an opportunity which none of them were ever likely to see again, and they were not going to let this slip through their fingers. However long it might take, they were determined to make a good job of the work for which they had been summoned. They were not going to be dictated to by anyone – least of all by a lot of old men trying to control everything from the dicasteries of the Vatican. Their father-in-God had told them that this was to be a Council of *Aggiornamento* and of *Ecumenismo* and they were prepared ruthlessly to destroy anything which stood in the way of this twofold hope.

[1] X. Rynne, *Letters from Vatican City*, p. 220.

CHAPTER FOUR

1963: *The People of God*

SHORTLY BEFORE 8 P.M. ON 3 JUNE, 1963, POPE
John died. There had been rumours that he was ill during the
First Session of the Council. Some said he had cancer; some
that he was to have an operation as soon as the First Session
came to an end; some that he ought to have an operation but
that it was impossible because he had a weak diaphragm; and
so on. No one seemed to know the truth. All one could say was
that, at eighty-one he looked remarkably tough whenever he
appeared in S. Peter's, and he survived unbelievably long and
tiring ceremonies with a fortitude which would have been com-
mendable in one half his age. But then he came of peasant
stock, of generations of tough little men who had managed, by
hard work and endurance, to wring a livelihood out of the
unrewarding soil of Sotto il Monte.

Just a month before he died I was in Rome on holiday and
paid a visit to S. Peter's. I found a considerable crowd up near
the high altar, and, when I enquired what was happening, I
was told that the Santo Padre was about to arrive in order to
greet a party of crippled children. And sure enough, within a
few minutes, the old man was carried in on his 'sedia gestatoria'
and placed in front of the children whom he addressed with a

firm, clear voice. As he was carried out, I noticed how pale he looked. Even this little excursion had obviously greatly tired him. Within a month he was dead.

If you elect a man of seventy-seven as your leader you naturally can't expect to have him for very long. Some would say that you can't really expect him to lead; but this would not be true of Pope John. In four and a half years he managed, in spite of his age, to change the whole course of Christian, if not of human, history. This he did, not by exercising great statesmanlike qualities, but by a curious, naïve simplicity, a kind of divine intuition mixed with considerable ignorance of what the world was like. I was amazed, for example, when I read his *Journal of a Soul*, to find him slipping up on quite elementary matters. For example, when he was Papal Representative at Istanbul, living close to the ancient and holy Orthodox Church, older than the Church of Rome, proud of its learning and its sanctity, he wrote: 'Very little is left in this land of the kingdom of Jesus Christ. Debris and seeds. But innumerable souls to be won for Christ, lost in this weltering mass of Moslems, Jews and Orthodox' – as if the members of the Orthodox Church were not even Christians.[1] Yet John instinctively knew that what the world wanted was love and simplicity, and he gave both with open arms.

In spite of some very odd statements, Pope John had a real concern for Christian Unity, though I doubt if he ever really understood the problems involved. Perhaps it was just because he didn't see the problems, that he was able to do what other people couldn't do. I think he realised that the old policy of the Church of Rome getting on with its own work and leaving the rest of the Christian world to find its way back into the fold, was not really going to work. What policy was to take its place, I doubt whether he, or anyone else, knew. But at least something ought to be done.

[1] *Journal of a Soul.* Tr. Dorothy White (London, 1965), p. 228.

Preaching at a Requiem for Pope John in the Anglican
Church of Holy Trinity, Leeds, on 11 June, I said:

'It is no good just sitting back and saying that the unity of all
Christians, which is so clearly the wish of our Blessed Lord, is only
a dream, something quite impossible of fulfilment and therefore to
be disregarded. If it is Christ's will that "all should be one", then
there must be a way through the deadlock into which we seem to
have drifted.

'When I was a boy I loved reading about the lumbermen in
Canada and of the great masses of logs drifting down the great
rivers. Occasionally the timber jammed, and I read of the lumber-
jacks leaping about on the logs, loosening one here and one there
until the whole great mass gradually started to grind its way
forward. I sometimes think of this as a parable of our present
condition. We have got into a jam, and it sometimes looks as if
there was no way out. But it is no good standing on the bank
and saying that the whole thing has got so tightly jammed that
there is nothing to be done. It needs someone to go out into
the middle of it and see whether he can get things moving.
It may not unlock the jam: what it can do is to create a different kind of jam, and out of that new pattern something may
emerge.

'That, I believe, is what Pope John did. He hasn't solved the
problem of Christian disunity. What he has done is to make it
into a *new* problem: and it is to that that we must now turn our
attention.'[1]

The death of the Pope threw the future of the Council into
some uncertainty. A Council can be summoned only by a Pope.
Much, therefore, would depend upon who the new Pope was
to be. Quite a lot of the cardinals disliked and disapproved of
the Council, and would have been quite glad to have heard the
end of it. If they had elected one who felt as they did, the Council
might have come to an untimely end with no decrees promulgated. But the momentum generated during the last four years
was too strong, and on 20 June we were informed that the

[1] Text in full in *The Tablet*, 15 June 1963.

Sacred College had elected Cardinal Montini, who had taken the title of Paul VI.

Everyone knew that Paul would be very different from John. He is much more of a scholar, much more of a statesman, much more cautious and calculating. A French bishop is said to have remarked: 'Only John could have started the Council: only Paul can finish it.' There is much truth in this. To start the Council at all needed a kind of reckless faith, which is just what John possessed. But to bring the Council to a successful conclusion would need some very careful and courageous leadership. Would Paul have the qualities needed? This was the question that everyone was asking during the summer of 1963.

No one really doubted that the Council would reassemble. After such a good start it would have been a great disaster if there had been no continuation of its work. Had the Council stopped at this point, it would have been regarded as a victory for the Curia and the more conservative elements. 'Look', they would have said, 'the irresponsible progressives have tried to wreck the Church; but fortunately the new Pope has stopped them.'

So, in due course, on Michaelmas Day, the Second Session of the Council opened.

At the opening service Pope Paul spoke for over an hour.[1] This was long; but it was important that he should say certain things to the vast assembly, who were naturally eager to know what he was thinking about some of the great problems which the Council would have to tackle. Of these problems, the greatest was that of the nature of the Church and its place in the world of today. The fathers would have to spend much time during the next few weeks discussing the Church, and the Pope reminded them that it would be their job 'to examine the in-

[1] The full text of his address is in X. Rynne, *The Second Session* (London, 1964), pp. 347-63.

timate nature of the Church and to express in human language, so far as that is possible, a definition which will best reveal the Church's real, fundamental constitution and make clear its manifold mission of salvation'.

What, precisely, *is* the Church? Of what does it consist? This question would have been a fairly simple one to answer in the early years of Christian history, when the Church was easy to define and to describe. It was the Christian community, whether local or universal, the fellowship of those who had accepted Christ as their Lord and Saviour, who were baptised, who worshipped together, who were united under acknowledged leaders, who lived a kind of life which was based on the teaching of Christ. But, today, things are much more uncertain and confused. Who can draw the boundaries of the Church of God today? Who can say who is in, and who is out?

The Prayer Book speaks of 'the blessed company of all faithful people'; but this is about as vague as it could be. Faithful in what? In their belief in God? or in Christ? Or does it mean those who accept the whole of the Nicene Creed? Are all those who accept the creeds necessarily within the Church?

Another Anglican formulary is a little more explicit. It says that 'the visible Church of Christ is a congregation of faithful men, in the which the pure Word of God is preached, and the Sacraments be duly ministered according to Christ's ordinance in all those things that of necessity are requisite to the same'. (Article XIX.) But this again begs a number of questions. Are the Sacraments 'duly ministered according to Christ's ordinance' in Churches where the Holy Communion is celebrated only three times a year, or in a Church which departs from the 'ordinance' of Christ by administering the Sacrament in one kind only?

Others don't believe in a 'visible Church' at all. To them the only kind of Church is a fellowship of the 'converted', the 'twice-born', those who are 'in Christ'. For such there can be no boundaries and no barriers. Only God knows who are members of his Church.

Or are we to adopt the theory once held by High Church Anglicans that the true Church is like a tree with three branches – Roman, Orthodox and Anglican? These are the communities which have preserved the ancient traditions and orders of the Church intact and, therefore, constitute the Church of God today.

Meanwhile, the Roman Catholic Church had always maintained that no one could claim to be a member of Christ's Church unless he was in communion with the see of Rome. These and these alone constituted the true Church; all others were outside. Some would say that, being outside the Church, they are destitute of all sacramental grace and without hope of salvation. Others, however, would prefer to leave that question open.

But, if the Council were, in Pope Paul's words, to produce 'a definition of the Church's real, fundamental constitution', then they would have to face this delicate question. They would also have to give considerable attention to the problem of Ecumenism and of the place in the divine economy of what they now politely termed the 'separated brethren'. Was there any way in which they could remain loyal to truth and yet hold out some hand of fellowship to the 'non-catholics' – Orthodox, Anglican, Protestant? The problem was indeed a difficult one. A desire for an ecumenical approach was now sweeping across large sections of the Church. Yet the Church had officially stated that 'the mystical body of Christ and the Roman Catholic Church are one and the same thing'.[1] Was there any way in which the Church could get round this difficulty?

This is what Paul said:

[1] From *Humani generis* (1950) in Denzinger, *Enchiridion Symbolorum* (Herder ed. 1953), No. 3019 on p. 709.

'The Council aims at complete and universal ecumenicity – that
is at least what it desires, what it prays and prepares for. Today
it does so in hope that tomorrow it may see the reality. The
Council, while calling and counting its own those sheep who belong to the fold of Christ in the fullest and truest sense, opens the
door and calls out also, in anxious expectation, to the many sheep
of Christ who are not at present within the unique fold.

'It is a council, therefore, of invitation, of expectation, of confidence, looking forward towards a more widespread, more
fraternal participation in its authentic ecumenicity.

'We speak now to the representatives of the Christian denominations separated from the Catholic Church, who have nevertheless been invited to take part as observers in this solemn assembly.
We greet them from our heart. We thank them for their participation. We transmit through them our message – as father and
brother – to the venerable Christian communities they represent.

'Our voice trembles and our heart beats faster both because of
the inexpressible consolation and reasonable hope that their
presence stirs up within us, as well as because of the deep sadness
we feel at their prolonged separation.

'If we are in any way to blame for that separation, we humbly
beg God's forgiveness and ask pardon too of our brethren who feel
themselves to have been injured by us. For our part, we willingly
forgive the injuries which the Catholic Church has suffered, and
forget the grief endured during the long series of dissensions and
separations. May the heavenly Father deign to hear our prayers
and grant us true, brotherly peace.'[1]

Nothing could have been more courageous than this. No
wonder that the Pope's voice trembled, for he must have known
that while greatly encouraging the observers he was deeply
offending many of his own friends. 'This unprecedented and
historic utterance', said Xavier Rynne, 'no doubt shocked
some of the fathers who have insisted that the Church is without
stain or blemish; but to the majority of the Pope's listeners it
was a great moment.'[2]

It was, indeed, a great moment, for it was, so far as I know,

[1] X. Rynne, *The Second Session*, pp. 357–8.   [2] *Ibid.*, p. 36.

the first occasion on which Rome had offered anything in the nature of an apology to other Christians. A year later, at the British Council of Churches' conference at Nottingham, an attempt was made to send a similar message to Rome, thanking the Pope and the Council for what they had done, and reciprocating the charitable and forgiving words which had been spoken. I regret to say that this suggestion was turned down, with acclamation from some members of the assembly. In the same spirit as Fr Ciappi, who declared that the Catholic Church 'has everything to give and nothing to receive',[1] so I fear there are some Protestants who believe that when it comes to expressions of remorse they have everything to receive and nothing to give.

The Second Session, although it ranged over many topics, was really concerned with one thing – the Church, the People of God, its nature, its constitution and its consistency. The first twenty-three full days were, therefore, devoted to the new Schema, *De Ecclesia*, with special reference to the authority of the Church and the relationship between the papacy and the episcopate. The Council then spent eight days talking about bishops and their function in the Church, before going on to spend the last eleven days discussing the problem of Ecumenism.

A draft on the Church had been presented at the First Session, but it had not made much progress. As we have seen, it came in for some heavy criticism and was sent back to the appropriate commission for revision. In fact, the commission soon discovered that they would really have to scrap the document which they had produced, and start again on something more likely to commend itself to the fathers.

The new Schema which was offered to the fathers in 1963 was considerably shorter than the previous document. After a brief introduction it contained only four chapters:

1. The Mystery of the Church.

[1] See above, p. 3.

2. The Hierarchical Constitution of the Church, with special
   reference to the Episcopate.
3. The People of God, and especially the Laity.
4. The Vocation to Holiness in the Church.

This was the document which was debated from 30 September
to 31 October, 1963 – the longest debate of any held during the
Council. As a result of the debate, the material was completely
rearranged, and certain new sections were added. In its revised
form the Schema consists of the following eight chapters:

1. The Mystery of the Church.
2. The People of God.
3. The Hierarchical Structure of the Church, and in
   particular the Episcopate.
4. The Laity.
5. The Universal Vocation to Holiness in the Church.
6. Religious.
7. The Eschatological Nature of the Pilgrim Church and its
   union with the Church in Heaven.
8. The Blessed Virgin Mary, Mother of God in the Mystery
   of Christ and the Church.

Much of this had appeared in the earlier Schema; but the
last chapter was a notable and important addition. One of the
most difficult problems which the Council had to face was what
to say about the Virgin Mary. During the last hundred years or
so two great dogmas had been promulgated – that of the Immaculate Conception in 1854, and that of the Assumption in
1950. These had greatly stimulated popular devotion in many
countries, and there was a demand from various quarters that
the Council should take things further and issue new decrees in
honour of our Lady. In sending in their suggestions a good
many of the bishops pleaded for new titles and honours to be
given to the Virgin, especially the designation of her as 'co-
redemptrix' and as 'mediatrix of all graces'.

In 1962 a Schema called 'De Beata Maria Virgine, Matre

Dei et Matre Hominum' had been circulated to the Council fathers. This had been prepared by the preparatory commission whose members, no doubt, realised that they had a fairly delicate task to perform, for it would obviously be extremely difficult to satisfy the two schools of thought among the fathers – those who wanted to begin with the new dogmas and go on from there, and those who wanted to go back to the biblical and patristic sources and try to produce something which would be more theological and, incidentally, more ecumenical. And this they had to do under the eagle eye of Pope John, whose devotion to our Lady was very deep and who had placed the whole Council under her protection.

The Commission, of course, knew that, among all the subjects which the Council would have to discuss, there was probably none more in danger of upsetting the observers and those whom they represented. Mariology and Mariolatry are very controversial matters, where the very excesses of the Roman Catholic Church have had the effect of driving many non-Romans to the other extreme – the excess of neglect. This, of course, is not true of the Orthodox Churches in which devotion to our Lady is strong and popular; but it is true of large parts of the Anglican Church and of Protestantism in general. There is reason for caution here, as many have observed. 'The evangelical', writes an Anglican, 'cannot but be impressed by what he sees in Roman churches: the blaze of candles throwing into relief shadowy figures praying before the statue of our Lady, while our Lord in the Blessed Sacrament is by comparison deserted';[1] while the Bishop of Cuernavaca in Mexico had to tell the Council that 'devotion to Mary and the saints, especially in our countries, at times obscures devotion to Christ'.[2] If

[1] J. de Satgé, 'Towards an Evangelical re-appraisal' in *The Blessed Virgin Mary: Essays by Anglican Writers*, ed. E. L. Mascall and H. S. Box (London, 1963), p. 106.

[2] X. Rynne, *The Second Session*, p. 49.

Roman Catholics have done great honour to our Lady by their devotion, they have also done some dishonour to her by making it so difficult for others to give her her due.

The Schema produced in 1962 began well enough with a number of quotations from the Bible indicating Mary's place and her co-operation in the divine plan. But it began to arouse suspicions in the minds of some of the observers when it began to speak of her as 'not only Mother of Jesus, the one and only divine Mediator and Redeemer, but also joined with him in carrying out the redemption of the human race'. Suspicion grew when it went on to speak to her as 'administrator and dis-penser of heavenly graces' and finally as 'mediatrix of all graces'. Nor were they comforted by the appended note which pointed out that these were not new phrases or titles since each of them had already appeared in some papal pronouncement, and that some of the expressions proposed by the 'maximalists' had been deliberately omitted. As for the title of 'co-redemp-trix', the note goes on to say that, although used by Pius X and Pius XI, it was left out of this Schema so as not to offend the 'separated brethren', though no attempt was made to dissociate the Council from this title or to throw any doubts upon its validity.

It was not only the protestant observers who felt some doubts about this Schema. Many of the fathers saw here a real danger that the Council might be jockeyed into making some declara-tion which would be regretted by those who were really working for the twofold purpose of renewal and reunion. The Schema was, therefore, studied with considerable misgiving. Although circulated during the First Session, it was never debated, though the fathers were invited to send in written suggestions and comments.

These suggestions and comments were printed in a booklet called 'Emendations', which was issued in 1963. It consists of 44 pages and includes 190 proposals. These show that the fathers were divided. Some felt that the Council was missing a great opportunity for making new dogmas about our Lady; some thought that even the cautious statements here made were likely to cause offence among non-Romans and ought, therefore, to be avoided. Meanwhile, a new question had been raised, which was whether or not any statement about the Blessed Virgin should be made a separate decree, or whether it should form part of a general constitution on the Church.

To this question the Council directed its attentions towards the end of October, 1963. No new Schema had yet been submitted, so that the fathers were not being asked to give their opinions on such things as 'Co-redemptrix' or 'Mediatrix of all graces'. What they were really being asked to do was to say whether they thought that our Lady should be treated as belonging to the Church or whether, in view of her exalted position, she should have special treatment.

The vote on this issue was, therefore, of great importance. No debate was held, but two speeches were made setting out the case for and against the publication of a separate Schema. This was on 24 October; and during the next few days prodigious efforts were made to try to persuade the fathers to vote for a separate document. Leaflets and counter-leaflets were distributed outside S. Peter's; rumours flew around as those most familiar with the ways of the Vatican studied the reports in the *Osservatore Romano* which tell the world who have been to see the Pope; attempts were even made to suggest that anyone voting against the idea of a separate Schema would be guilty of insulting the Virgin Mother.

The vote was not taken until 29 October, when we were informed that whereas 1,074 had declared their wish for a separate and independent Schema, 1,114 thought that any statement about our Lady should be included in the constitution on the Church. This was the closest vote ever taken in the Council. A mere handful of votes (twenty-one in all) would have turned the thing the other way, with results which might have proved disastrous. Many of the observers wondered if this was a sign that the Holy Spirit was at work.

After the vote the Commission for the constitution on the Church could get to work on the chapter which was to deal with the Blessed Virgin. This was a new text altogether, and one far more satisfactory in view of the purposes for which the Council had been called. In its final form it was greeted by all but the most protestant of the observers as a just and unexceptionable statement which could not reasonably be accused of raising new barriers among the people of God. Certain titles are attributed to the Virgin – Advocate, Supporter, Helper, Mediator – but the two expressions most likely to cause offence ('co-redemptrix' and 'mediatrix of all graces') were carefully avoided, and those titles which are used are carefully safeguarded from possible misinterpretation by the statement:

> 'This, however, is to be understood that it neither takes away from, nor adds anything to, the dignity and efficaciousness of Christ, the one Mediator. For no creature could ever be counted equal with the incarnate Word and Redeemer. Just as the priesthood of Christ is shared in various ways both by the ministers and by the faithful, and as the one goodness of God is really communicated in different ways to his creatures, so also the unique mediation of the Redeemer does not exclude, but rather gives rise to a manifold co-operation which is but a sharing in this one source. The Church does not hesitate to profess this subordinate rôle of Mary. It knows it through unfailing experience of it, and commends it to the hearts of the faithful, so that, encouraged by this material help, they may the more intimately adhere to the Mediator and Redeemer.'

No doubt many of the fathers found all this very unsatisfactory and perhaps even thought it disrespectful. But, as Fr Congar writes, it 'all springs from the gulf that exists between the "return-to-sources" Catholicism which is, by the same token, Catholicism wholly centred on Christ, and also biblical, liturgical, paschal, community-minded, ecumenical and missionary, and that Catholicism which ignores these sources, and within which specialised teams are devoted to obtaining the maximum "development" of certain Mariological propositions.'[1] Abbot Butler, whose opinions carry great weight in both Roman and non-Roman fields, writes: 'I can only say that I personally believe that devotion to our Lady will gain in quality through the Council's resolution to "contain" Marian doctrine within the framework of the theology of her divine Son and of the Church of which she is both type and "pre-eminent member".'[2]

Now that the Roman Church has done so much to try to 'contain' its Mariology, it is to be hoped that non-Roman Churches may be encouraged to take another look at their teaching on this important subject. In the past the tendency has been to be negative or to ignore the matter altogether. But this is not good enough. When the Anglican Prayer Book was finally settled in 1662 its calendar included five feasts of our Lady, two of red-letter status (Annunciation and Purification) and three of lesser solemnity (Conception, Nativity and Visitation). In the previous century the Church had been more cautious. There was much superstition in England in the later Middle Ages, and the reformers, while anxious to retain a sound theology about our Lady, were determined to purge the country of an excessive and un-biblical popular devotion. Their policy succeeded; for in the seventeenth century, while there was no flamboyant Mariolatry, there was some sound Mariology, as, for example, that expressed in Thomas Ken's hymn: 'Her Virgin-eyes saw God incarnate born'.[3] The Tractarians also, and their successors, naturally adopted a certain amount of Roman Catholic phrase-

[1] Yves Congar, O.P., *Report from Rome II* (London, 1964), p. 82.

[2] *De Ecclesia: The Constitution on the Church of Vatican Council II*, ed. Gregory Baum (London, 1965), p. 11.

[3] See A. M. Allchin, 'Our Lady in Seventeenth-century Anglican Devotion and Theology' in E. L. Mascall and H. S. Box, *op. cit.* p. 53–76.

ology both in their teaching and in their worship. But there still exists a certain amount of suspicion and confusion in Anglican thought – as I once heard a preacher say: 'You know, the trouble is that you all think that our Lady was a Roman Catholic'.

The excesses of Rome have certainly led to neglect elsewhere, and this should be remedied. What we need is a positive and theological approach to the subject, to forget about the grottoes and the processions, the visions and the fables, the sickly statuettes and the 'seven swords stuck in her heart', and try to see the place of Mary in the divine plan of man's redemption.

If the Son of God was to become Man, then someone must give him his human body and his human nature. Only one person could do this, and the person whom God selected for this purpose would be unique among all human beings who have ever lived. But, since man has free will, God's plan depended upon the willing co-operation of the woman whom he had chosen. When the message was conveyed to Mary that God was inviting her to act with him in this way, she could have refused. As I have written elsewhere: 'Mary's consent was necessary if God's plan was to be fulfilled. Even at this moment of God's intervention he depended upon the help of a girl; and, for an instant, between the last words of the angel and Mary's response, the purpose and plan of God hung in the air, and the whole hope of man's redemption was in suspense. Will she respond? Will she accept this awe-full responsibility? Will she agree to be the mother of the Lord?'[1] By giving her consent Mary has played a unique part in our redemption. To call her 'co-redemptrix' would be to use too strong a word since it might seem to throw doubt on the uniqueness and fullness of Christ's work as Redeemer; and yet it clearly expresses a truth in that 'Mary's *Fiat* was the act of human obedience which reversed the whole pattern of human disobedience and so made

[1] John Moorman, *The Path to Glory* (London, 1960), p. 10.

it possible for God to set in operation his work of recreating the human race'.[1]

At the end of the Third Session, in 1964, Pope Paul conferred upon Mary a new title when he called her 'Mother of the Church'. This was something of a shock and a disappointment, not only to the observers but to many of the fathers who feared that it would undo something of what they had so carefully done in their statement on our Lady. It looked as if, after all, the Pope was going to override the wishes of the Council and declare a new dogma. But this was not so. The designation 'Mother of the Church' is not a new dogma, it is only a title, and, surely, not one to which great exception can be taken. It can, for example, be argued that if the Church is the Body of Christ, and if Mary gave Christ his body, then it can reasonably be said that Mary is the Mother of the Church. Or we may link it with Christ's last words to Mary and John from the Cross: 'Woman, behold thy son. . . . Behold thy mother,' and say with Dr Lightfoot: 'Mary, the Lord's physical mother now becomes, at the Lord's bidding and as a result of his work, the spiritual mother of all those who are to be born in him.'[2] If the Church is the fellowship of those 'reborn in Christ' – as the Evangelicals say – then there is a proper sense in which Mary can be called the Mother of the Church.

When I was discussing the Council with a group of monks at Ampleforth early in 1963 they asked me:

'What surprised you most about the Council?'

'That it should have been held at all.'

'Why did you feel that?'

'Because', I replied, 'I had always looked upon Vatican I as likely to be the last of the series, the Council to end all Councils. For Vatican I attempted to settle the problem which was raised by Marsiglio of Padua in the fourteenth century and was

[1] E. L. Mascall in Mascall & Box, *op. cit.*, p. 20.

[2] R. H. Lightfoot, *S. John's Gospel: A Commentary* (Oxford, 1956), p. 320.

debated all through the fifteenth century – namely, which is
the highest authority: Pope or Council? But surely after 1870
there can be no problem here. If the Pope is infallible, then
what is a Council for? If he wants advice he can get it. If he
doesn't want advice he can manage perfectly well without it.
So why bother to call a Council?'

But the fathers thought differently. To them Vatican II was
inevitable even though it had taken nearly a century to
summon it. Vatican I had, indeed, declared in favour of Papal
Infallibility; but it had been cut short in its work by the inva-
sion of Rome in 1870, and many things which it intended to do
had not been done. One of its intentions was to go on to discuss
the place of the bishops (or should we say 'the rest of the
bishops'?) in the Church. But this had never been done.
Vatican II was, therefore, the natural sequence to Vatican I,
and one of its most important jobs would be to give some kind of
ruling as to the authority of the episcopate.

The good monks were in fact right. Vatican II did feel the
necessity of facing this problem, and a good deal of time was
taken up in discussing it. From 4 to 16 October, and again for
several days in November, the Council fathers wrestled with
this problem.

There is no doubt that Christ chose the twelve apostles and
trained them in order that they might become the nucleus of
the Church, the natural leaders who would direct the affairs
of the Church when he was no longer with them in bodily form.

There is no doubt that Christ made Peter the head of this
apostolic team.

There was no doubt in their minds (though there is considerable doubt in some of ours) that, as Peter was to become the
founder of the Church in Rome, Christ intended all future
Bishops of Rome to inherit that position of leadership of divine
right in perpetuity.

There was no doubt in their minds that the Roman Pontiff is

the final authority in all matters of faith and morals and that he has power over every member of the Church.

There was no doubt in the minds of many of them that this power, as exercised by the Curia, made the life of a modern bishop very difficult.

The questions, therefore, which the Council had to decide were: 'What is a bishop?' 'What authority does he exercise?' 'How do the bishops as a whole stand in relation to the Pope?'

Pope Paul in his opening address had said that the first matter which the Council would have to consider was: 'taking for granted the dogmatic declaration of the First Vatican Council regarding the Roman Pontiff, to develop the doctrine regarding the episcopate, its function and its relationship with Peter'. By way of helping the fathers to tackle this problem he let fall the word 'collaboration'. But if the Pope and the bishops were to collaborate in the government of the Church, then the bishops must somehow manage to organise themselves into some form of corporate body. So arose the words 'college' and 'collegiality' which formed the basis of this long debate.

The bishops had to begin by studying the nature of episcopal consecration. This was a subject which had been debated for a very long time. Some theologians had held that consecration to the episcopate raises a man to a higher order than that of the priest. But this had been denied. The greatest thing which a man can do is to celebrate the Eucharist. By so doing he is able to change the bread and wine, so that they become the Body and Blood of Christ, and to offer the Eucharistic Sacrifice to God. Power to do this is given to a man when he is ordained as priest, and there is nothing of greater honour than this. A bishop is, therefore, a priest to whom extra authority has been given – the government of a diocese, the power to ordain the men who will offer the Eucharistic Sacrifice and to confirm the people who will receive the Sacrament at his hands.

But you could hardly expect the 2,000 bishops at the Council to accept this. The first question, therefore, which they had to discuss was the meaning of episcopal consecration: was it a sacramental act, conferring on them the highest degree of sacramental order? or was it a juridical act giving them status and function in the Church? If they agreed that consecration was a sacramental act, and that they were not just priests with additional jurisdiction, then they would be able to look upon themselves as a distinct body in the Church, the modern counterpart of the apostolic team. Such a body could be called a 'college' and would be what the lawyers would call a 'corporation aggregate'; and, as such, it would have to enter into some kind of relationship with the papacy, which would be called a 'corporation sole'. But, in working out this relationship, the bishops would have to decide whether they believed that they owed their position to the Pope or whether they held it of divine right.

These were the problems which the Council fathers had to tackle, and it soon became clear that there was a deep cleavage between them. One party wanted to put the power of the papacy into the context of the total jurisdiction and authority of the Church. Such authority would be exercised by the episcopate as a whole, working 'under Peter' or, better still, 'with Peter', just as in the Primitive Church the apostles acted together. They thus wanted the episcopate, including the Pope as *primus inter pares*, to become a joint source of authority. In order that the episcopate might express its opinions and collaborate with the Pope, they wanted some kind of senate or representative body, meeting regularly in Rome to advise the Pope and assist him in making decisions.

But this course did not satisfy all of them. Some saw this as a direct attack on the unique position of the Roman Pontiff as defined at Vatican I. Many of them saw it as a threat to the Curia, that comparatively small body of men, of whom only a few were bishops, who lived in Rome and controlled the affairs of the Church down to the smallest detail. The whole idea of 'collegiality' filled them with foreboding. If you once let the democratic principle creep into the affairs of the Church, then you were doomed. The whole power of the Church would crumble and dissolve.

Such was the cleavage of opinion which ran right through the Council during the October debates on the Church. No less than 191 speeches were delivered on this subject, so that practically every conceivable point was made – practical, judicial, theological, and ecumenical. The more conservative and curially-minded element put up a strong fight against the idea of Collegiality, which seemed to them to be a real threat to the infallibility of the Pope and to the power of the Curia, which they regarded as the greatest power for good in the life of the Church. Some were obviously uncertain as to what the term 'Collegiality' really meant, or what a College of Bishops would look like. A story which circulated in Rome during the debate said that Cardinal Cushing had asked one morning what the fathers had been discussing. When told that the subject was 'Collegiality', he asked: 'What's that?' 'They want a College of Bishops', was the reply. 'Ah,' he said, 'now I understand. Well, if they want a College of Bishops here in Rome tell 'em I'll raise a million dollars to get it built.'

As the battle was fought out, it became more and more clear that those who supported the idea of Collegiality were going to win the day. The climax came at the end of October when the moderators put four leading questions to the fathers in order to discover what the mind of the Council really was. The four questions were as follows:

1. Is the Schema to be drawn up in such a way that it states that episcopal consecration constitutes *the highest degree of the sacramental order?*

2. Is the Schema to be drawn up in such a way that it states that every bishop lawfully consecrated in communion with

the bishops and the Roman Pontiff (who is their head and the source of unity) is a member of *the body* of bishops?

3. Is the Schema to be drawn up in such a way that it states that the body or *college of bishops is the successor of the apostles* in the office of preaching the Gospel, sanctifying and tending their flocks, and that it enjoys *full and sovereign authority over the whole Church*, together with its head the Roman Pontiff and never without this head (whose right of primacy over all pastors and all the faithful remains untouched and whole)?

4. Is the Schema to be drawn up in such a way that it states that the above-mentioned power belongs to the college of bishops in union with its head, by *divine right?*[1]

All these questions were carried by large majorities. As each question was put, over 2,100 of the Council fathers voted; but, for the first question only 34 dissentients were found, for the second 104, for the third 336 and for the fourth 408. Thus was won a great victory for the principle of Collegiality and all that it meant.

We in the observers' box received this with considerable satisfaction since the whole issue had obvious ecumenical implications. We welcomed it as a corrective to the doctrine of Papal Infallibility, which can now be seen in proportion. Authority in future will rest not with the Pope alone but with the episcopate, the apostles, together with their leader. But the faithful have the right to demand guidance and, indeed, positive statements on problems of faith and of morals. It will in future be the responsibility of the whole episcopate (*cum Petro*, or, if you prefer it, *sub Petro*) to give this guidance and to make the authoritative decisions. But bishops are fallible and may disagree. Indeed no one could sit for a single morning as an observer and not find *that* out. On a really controversial

---

[1] Yves Congar, *Report from Rome II*, pp. 91–2; X. Rynne, *The Second Session*, pp. 170–1.

subject it might happen that the bishops were equally divided. In that case, of course, the Pope would have to give the casting vote, beyond which there could obviously be no appeal. In this way authority, which is spread out over the whole episcopate, is gradually narrowed down until, in the last resort, the Pope has to make the final decision. In so doing, it is reasonable to suppose that the Holy Spirit would not allow him to go wrong. Looked at in this way, the old bugbear of Papal Infallibility looked a little less alarming.

Secondly, this long debate did much to undermine the power of the Curia, a power long resented by bishops all over the world. The conditions in which the Church has to do its work are changing so rapidly that any bishop who has imagination and courage knows that he must make experiments, take risks, make snap decisions on the outcome of which much will depend. More and more of the bishops, especially those in the mission field, were becoming increasingly irritated at having to submit their problems to a group of men in Rome, many of whom could have little knowledge of the conditions in which people lived in the heart of Africa or the islands of the Pacific, and who tended to base their judgments on text-books and precedents.

Thirdly, the idea of Collegiality was a great encouragement to the bishops. Life can be very lonely for a man working in some vast diocese with only a handful of priests. It is easy to get depressed, frustrated, discouraged. But under the new principle they will know that, however isolated and remote they may be, they have some say in the affairs of the Church as a whole, and this by divine right (*jure divino*). 'The bishops', wrote a Lutheran observer, 'are not mere messenger-boys for the Pope and the Curia, nor merely executive secretaries of the ecclesiastical corporation on the diocesan level, but men who, by their epis-copal consecration, have responsibility and authority both for the diocese and for the entire Church.'[1] When the results of the

[1] *Dialogue on the Way*, ed. G. A. Lindbeck (Minneapolis, 1965), p. 53.

voting on the 'guiding questions' became known, many of the bishops felt at least six inches taller.

Meanwhile there was a fifth question, of an entirely different nature, which was also passed by a comfortable majority of three to one. This concerned the diaconate and asked whether this should be restored as 'a distinct and permanent degree of the sacred ministry in accordance with the needs of the Church in various regions'. This seems a fairly harmless suggestion, but, in fact, it led to a heated debate in which the world press got itself involved. The reason for this was that in § 15 of the Schema under discussion there were a few sentences on deacons which, after outlining what a deacon was entitled to do, and suggesting that in certain parts of the world a permanent diaconate should be established, said that it would be for the ecclesiastical authorities to decide whether or not such deacons should be 'bound by the sacred law of celibacy'. This was the first point at which sex crept into the Vatican Council, and it whipped up considerable controversy both within S. Peter's and outside.

The demand for permanent deacons had come from those parts of the world where there is a great shortage of clergy, especially South America. The mission of the Church is, in these countries, very much hampered and delayed because there are so few priests. There are, however, men who, without feeling any vocation to the priesthood, could be used by the Church in teaching, baptising, pastoral visiting and so forth. Such men would be encouraged in their ministry if they could receive holy orders, i.e. as deacons. But this raised the question as to whether the diaconate could be conferred on a married man. For the last thousand years or so the Roman Catholic Church has imposed the rule of celibacy on all its bishops, priests and deacons. To relax this discipline would mean a considerable change in the Church's whole attitude to the ministry, and many of the bishops were not at all happy about the suggestion.

On the other hand, unless these permanent deacons were allowed to marry, the plan would, to some extent, break down. For, if these men were required to remain unmarried for the rest of their lives, the number of applicants would be small; and, if they were prepared to accept the rule of celibacy, there would seem little point in their not becoming priests. The whole plan, therefore, turned on this question, and all the old arguments were trotted out.

As the Roman Catholic Church is the only Church in the world which imposes a rule of celibacy on all its clergy, everyone in the observers' box came from a Church which has a married clergy (if they have any clergy at all), and we were naturally interested to see which way the debate would go. It was pretty clear that the bishops from South America, where the need is greatest,[1] were in favour of married deacons, as they saw here a chance of enrolling men to carry the Church's work into places where otherwise there would be no mission owing to the extreme shortage of priests. On the other hand, bishops from countries which are still pretty well stocked with priests were much more alarmed at this proposal, though even they must realise that the number of men offering themselves for ordination is going down rapidly.

When the Schema on the Church was finally passed, the passage on deacons read as follows: 'The diaconate in future can be restored as a proper and permanent rank of the hierarchy.... With the consent of the Roman Pontiff this diaconate can, in the future, be conferred upon men of more mature age, even upon those living in the married state'.

The debate on the Church virtually ended on 31 October, though, as always, a few extra speeches were made as bishops claimed the right to speak on behalf of large, regional groups.

[1] It appears that in South America there is one priest to every 5,000 baptised Catholics, whereas in some European countries the proportion is one to every 500: *Herder Correspondence* (1965), p. 362.

By this time a great many subjects had been talked about – In-
fallibility, Primacy of Peter, Collegiality of bishops, the Blessed
Virgin Mary, Eschatology, the Missionary task of the Church,
Church and State, non-Catholics, non-Christians, Atheism, the
Jews, Lapsed Catholics, Poverty and Wealth, Priesthood, the
Diaconate, Celibacy, Papal legates and nuncios, acolytes, the
laity, family life, the priesthood of the faithful, women in the
Church, racial discrimination, etc. etc. Out of this welter of
material the Commission had to try to produce something on
which the fathers could vote. This they did in September, 1964,
when the final draft went through without much difficulty and
was finally promulgated on 21 November.

This constitution, generally known as 'Lumen Gentium' from
its opening words, is a remarkable piece of work. As Abbot
Butler says: 'I have no hesitation in saying that the Constitution
is a great document,'[1] It lays the theological foundations for
many of the subjects which were to be discussed later on – the
Priesthood, the Laity, the Religious Orders, Ecumenism and the
Church in the Modern World. To continue what Christopher
Butler says: 'Its worth for the Church and for the future of
Christianity will depend largely on our willingness to understand and communicate its message and to give practical expression to its implications. Its key doctrines are: the common
priesthood of all the faithful, originating in their baptism; the
intrinsic life of the local Church, centred in the eucharist and
the ministerial priesthood and episcopate; and the collegial
authority and responsibilities of the bishops within the heir-
archical communion of the Church.'[2]

After the long debate on the Church, so much of which had

[1] *De Ecclesia: The Constitution on the Church of Vatican Council II*, with a
Foreword by the Abbot of Downside and a Commentary by Gregory Baum,
O.S.A. (London, 1965), p. 8.
[2] But see a Protestant criticism of it by Professor Skydsgaard in *Dialogue
on the Way*, pp. 145–74.

been concerned with the place which bishops occupied in the structure of the Church, the Council took up a draft entitled 'On Bishops and the Government of Dioceses'. This, like the other documents, had been prepared by a preparatory commission; but it soon became known that, after the commission had completed its work, and its members had gone back to their dioceses, a handful of people in Rome had largely altered the text of the document to bring it more into line with the ideas of the Curia. How they hoped to get away with this is beyond comprehension, for the members of the commission were bound to come back and reveal what had happened. 'The text as we now have it is certainly not the one drawn up by the preparatory commission', said Bishop Gargitter of Bressanone. Bishop Rupp of Monaco informed the Council that the original text 'had undergone several surgical operations'.[1] And the attempts made by the arch-conservative Bishop Carli of Segni (who was popularly supposed to be the mouthpiece of Ottaviani and the Holy Office) to justify what had taken place did not ring true.

The trouble about the Schema now before the fathers was that it was totally out of keeping with what the Council had just decided—about Collegiality and the rights of the episcopate to do their job without being pestered by the Curia. So, what with the accusations of 'dirty work' in the Curia and the new liberty which the fathers had just won for themselves, the debate on this Schema turned out to be one of the most acrimonious.

It lasted from 5 to 15 November, and really turned into three things: a continuation of the debate on Collegiality, a demand for an episcopal senate or synod to assist the Pope, and an attack on the Curia. On all these subjects many of the bishops felt strongly, and some of them thought that the Council had been let down. It was, in fact, not so much a clash of policies as of personalities – Frings and Ottaviani being the two most concerned. Both are well over seventy and nearly blind, but they

[1] X. Rynne, *The Second Session*, p. 174.

are both 'bonny fighters'. Frings said openly, what a good many
of the bishops felt, that the methods and behaviour of the Holy
Office were a cause of scandal to the world, which soon brought
Ottaviani to his feet accusing Frings of ignorance and, indeed,
of making a personal assault on the Pope who is, technically,
the head of the Holy Office.

It soon became clear that the Council was not prepared to
accept the mutilated text which had been offered to it, and the
debate ended on 15 November with the draft being sent back
for revision. When it reappeared in 1964 it had been completely rewritten in a far more peaceful and pastoral tone under
the title of 'The Pastoral Office of Bishops in the Church'.[1]

Since the general theme of the Second Session was 'the
People of God', the Council knew that sooner or later it would
have to come to grips with the problem as to where this body
of people was to be found. Was it to be identified with the
Roman Catholic Church? or were other Christians in some way
eligible for membership? In the Constitution on the Church the
fathers had been asked to declare that there is only one Church
and that 'this Church, the true Mother and Teacher of all, constituted and appointed in this world as a society, is the Catholic
Church governed by the Roman Pontiff and by bishops in communion with him'; but they had jibbed at this and changed it to
'this Church, founded and organised in this world as a society,
has its existence in the Catholic Church under the government
of Peter's successor and the bishops in communion with him',
adding that 'outside her framework there are found many
elements of holiness and truth which give an impetus to
universal unity inasmuch as they are gifts which belong to
Christ's Church'.

The problems of 'non-Catholics', of obvious Christians who
are not members of the Roman Church, comes up again in the

[1] See below, pp. 112–14.

same Constitution which states that 'with all those who, having been baptised, are adorned with the name of Christ, but who do not profess the whole faith nor share in unity under the Roman Pontiff, the Church, as a loving mother of all, knows herself to be in many ways joined'. Some of these Christians, having been baptised, have a deep faith in the mystery of the Eucharist and great devotion towards the Blessed Virgin – an obvious reference to the Eastern Orthodox Churches which have almost everything in common with Rome, except submission to the papacy.

Observers read all this with some degree of satisfaction. The Schema seemed to be groping for some form of words which would recognise the very obvious Christian qualities of those who were not in communion with Rome. But it was pointed out that, although the Schema tries to be polite about 'non-Catholics', it is really thinking in terms of individuals, since it makes no reference to other Churches in which these qualities are pre-eminent. There is still, therefore, some indication that the Church of Rome is thinking of herself as the mother of the prodigal son, opening her arms to welcome into his home anyone who, for various reasons, has strayed from her. This is not altogether in keeping with the hospitable and understanding words with which Pope Paul had opened the Second Session when he had referred to 'venerable Christian communities' and to 'other Christian bodies distinguished by the name of Church' which were not in communion with Rome, and had even said that 'among the different components of the visible and mystical body are the Separated Brethren'.

How far can 'non-Catholics' be regarded as members of the visible and Mystical Body of Christ which is the Church? This was a question which haunted the minds of the Council fathers throughout the Second Session when they were discussing the two questions which are so closely related – that of the Church and that of Ecumenism.

At the back of their minds was a feeling that, if a person is baptised in water and in the name of the Trinity, he must be, in some way, incorporated into Christ and so, as our Articles say, be 'grafted into the Church'. There was, indeed, some solid ground for this belief, for in *Mediator Dei* (1947) Pius XII had officially declared that those who are validly baptised become 'by a common title members of Christ the Priest'[1]; and, before the Council, Cardinal Bea had gone about saying that 'the Catholic Church affirms resolutely the general doctrine of the New Testament that, through valid baptism, even though it is conferred outside the Roman Catholic Church, the baptised person is organically united with Christ and his Mystical Body'.[2]

Having, then, laid down certain foundation-stones in the Constitution on the Church, the fathers could turn to consider once more the problem of Ecumenism, of the relations between the Roman Catholic Church and the rest of the Christian world.

The Schema offered to the Council in 1962 had been a failure.[3] It was far too limited in its scope and far too narrow in its approach. Now an entirely new document had been drawn up, not by the Commission on the Eastern Churches, but by the Secretariat for Unity; and it was this which was laid before the fathers on 18 November, 1963. The draft consisted of three chapters:

1. The principles of Catholic Ecumenism.
2. The Practice of Ecumenism.
3. Christians separated from the Catholic Church:
    (a) The Eastern Churches;
    (b) Christian Communities arising from the 16th Century onwards.

Later on two other chapters were added, one on the Jews and

---

[1] Denzinger, *Enchiridion*, No. 3000.
[2] A. Bea, *The Unity of Christians* (London, 1963), p. 83.
[3] See above, pp. 56–8.

one on Religious Liberty, though what precisely these had to do with Ecumenism was not very clear.

Chapter 1, on the theory of Ecumenism, seemed to us to be reasonably good. It had a good passage expressing what Bea and others had so often said about Baptism, and what had been more or less agreed upon in the Constitution on the Church. The sentence now ran as follows: 'Brethren who believe in Christ and have received valid baptism, but who do not enjoy full communion with the Church, are nevertheless joined to us in a kind of communion. Those baptised in Christ Jesus are justly adorned with the name of Christ, and the Church recognises them as sons.' The same paragraph went on to show that Christians of all denominations have a great deal in common – a fact which needs emphasising in all ecumenical dialogue. All this was, of course, very cautious and guarded; but we were led to suppose that the framers of the draft decree had expected a great deal of opposition, and they had to be careful.

Chapter 2 pointed out what Pope John had always said, that the first step which any Church can take towards unity is one of reform and renewal of itself. The first part of this chapter, therefore, pointed out that there was a good deal within the Church which needed to be reformed before she could expect others to look towards her with much longing. Catholics must face the question of their part in Christian Unity with humility, as Pope Paul had recently reminded them. But, having said all this, the chapter goes on to suggest ways in which Roman Catholics can join in the work and prayer for unity in which the rest of Christendom has been for many years so deeply involved. Here the draft is more adventurous. Those who drew it up realised that the old idea of the Roman Church just sitting tight and expecting the rest of Christendom to come penitently back was hopelessly unrealistic. No move towards unity could come without co-operation, dialogue, encounter, confrontation.

D

The decree, therefore, says that, 'in special circumstances, such as prayer-meetings for unity and in ecumenical conferences, Catholics are allowed, and indeed encouraged, to join with their separated brethren in prayer'. It lays upon all Catholics the duty of finding out more about their fellow-Christians, declares that teaching about the non-Roman Churches shall be given in colleges and seminaries, and demands co-operation between the different Churches in the mission field. All this, of course, was very different from Ottaviani's instructions in 1949 which had declared that 'the Catholic Church takes no part in ecumenical conferences or meetings', and had warned the bishops that only the Catholic version of the history of the Reformation was to be taught, that true reunion can come about only by the return of dissidents to the one, true Church of Christ, that no prayers may be said together except the Lord's Prayer and other prayers specifically approved by the Catholic Church, and that if any theological discussions take place the Holy Office must be informed of the questions discussed, the names of those present and of the speakers on both sides.[1] Since all this had been said, on high authority, only fourteen years before, it was no wonder that members of the Secretariat feared a rough passage for their draft Schema.

The first part of Chapter 3, dealing with the Eastern Churches, was warm in its praise of their worship, their spirituality, their monastic life, and so on; but the second part, which was entitled 'Christian Communities arising from the 16th Century onwards', set off to a bad start. As soon as the Anglican delegates read this they told the members of the Secretariat for Unity that they thought it a pity that the Anglican Church had been omitted from the Schema. It was clearly not one of the Oriental Churches, but equally clearly it could not be said to have 'arisen' in the 16th century, since it was the ancient Church of the English people, catholic but reformed. The point

[1] G. K. A. Bell, *Documents on Christian Unity*, iv, pp. 22–6.

was noted and, in due course, the title of this sub-chapter was changed.

The additional chapters, one entitled 'On the Jews and other non-Christians', and the other 'On Religious Liberty', were introduced later in the session and immediately created considerable interest. But there was no time to discuss either of them adequately, and in the end they had to be carried over to the following year.

The debate on Ecumenism, when it could be kept off either the Jews or Religious Liberty, revealed very clearly the two fundamentally opposite views on Christian Unity held by members of the Council. One was the view that there was really no problem at all. The unity which Christ willed already exists in the (Roman) Catholic Church. The question, therefore, is how to persuade those outside to come in. Whether they come singly or in battalions doesn't really matter, so long as they come. Those who held this view dislike talk about penitence and humility. If anyone needed to be humble and penitent it was the poor sinner who had wandered away from the true Church or who, having been born outside it, delayed his return home. Bishop Muldoon, coadjutor of Sydney, put this point of view with good, colonial bluntness. 'We deceive ourselves', he said, 'if we think that all our separated brethren are in good faith. Many of them are like eagles, hovering over the Church, looking for what they can distort.' He was tired, he said, of all this talk about penitence. 'Some', he said, 'have declared that the bishops should all go down on their knees and confess their sins and those of their predecessors for the division of Christendom, and they quote the words of Pope Paul. But the Pope only said "*if* we are in any way to blame, etc." Saving his reverence, some of us are tired of this constant attempt to get at us. If any bishops feel guilty about it, let them go to a good confessor, but leave us alone.' The Archbishop of Bari asked why, since heretics and schismatics are outside the Church, it can be said

that they share 'a certain communion' with those inside; and a
Spanish bishop told the fathers that no doubt the separated
brethren were sincere in what they believed but that didn't
make the slightest difference to the necessity for them to give
up their foolish ways and come into the 'true Church'.

It is, perhaps, only fair to say that some of the prelates who
expressed opinions such as these may be excused on the grounds
of ignorance and fear. Many of them know very little about
'non-Catholics'. They never meet them or have any conversation with them. They think of them as traitors and deserters
who remain outside the Roman communion at their own peril.
Many of these bishops also have a very real fear of 'indifferentism'. They believe that the Roman Church has survived just
because it has been definite in its teaching. In dialogue and discussion with non-Romans they see the danger of the pure
truths being adulterated, of a drift towards 'pan-Christianity', of
syncretism, of encouraging a feeling that it doesn't matter
which Church you belong to as we are all going to the same
place. This is a very real fear, and one which is not confined to
members of the Roman Catholic Church.

On the other side were those who really wanted this Council
to make some progress towards better and closer relations
between the Roman Communion and the rest of the Christian
world. They realised that the exclusive attitude as expressed in
the 1949 Instructions was something which was now out-of-
date. The Church had stood aside long enough. The hour had
now come for her to become involved in the Ecumenical Movement which was sweeping across the world. But, if she was to do
that, then she must begin by setting her own house in order.
Some of her prelates might think that the Church looked 'without spot or wrinkle' to those outside; but they knew well enough
that this was not true. Abbot Reetz, Superior General of the
Benedictines of Beuron in Germany, gave the Council some
idea of what protestant theologians from Tübingen had told

him. 'One of their major complaints', he said, 'was what we might call our contorted and acrobatic theology – such as the volume, printed with ecclesiastical authority, arguing for the Immaculate Conception of S. Joseph and his assumption into heaven'. Similarly, he said, they dislike excessive scholasticism in our theology, undue juridicism in our dealings with one another, and certain forms of piety, such as the 'Rosary of the Tears of Mary', which can only obscure true devotion. There was, he thought, very urgent need of reform and renewal. If the fathers thought that they could go on like this without doing anything about it, then indeed they would need to get down on their knees.

But perhaps the most striking speech on this subject was that made by Bishop Stephen Leven, auxiliary of San Antonio in Texas. He started off by saying that, from what had been said in the Council, anyone might think that there was only one text in the Holy Bible – *Matthew* 16: 18: 'Thou art Peter and upon this rock I will build my Church'! 'Again and again in this *aula*', he said, 'they continue to chastise us, as if the prelate who feels compelled by clear evidence to acknowledge the gifts of the Holy Spirit in persons of other ecclesiastical bodies were denying the Faith and giving scandal to the innocent. They prefer to blame non-Catholics, whom perhaps they have never seen, than to instruct the children in their parishes. Otherwise, why are they so afraid the effects of ecumenism would not be good?' 'It seems', he continued, 'the dangers arising from ecumenism may be exaggerated. The prelates who seek a sincere and fruitful dialogue with non-Catholics are not the ones who show disaffection and disloyalty to the Holy Father. It is not our people who miss Mass on Sunday, refuse the sacraments and vote the Communist ticket'.[1]

This sort of tough, outspoken language showed that some of the Council fathers were determined to get the Church moving

[1] *Council Speeches of Vatican II* (London, 1964), pp. 100–02.

in the ecumenical world. That this was not just a question of waiting for the others to come in was stated over and over again. One of the points made was that dialogue must be on the footing of equality and not *de haut en bas*, this being made clear by Fr Fernandez, Master General of the Dominican Order, who warned the Council against the fallacy of thinking that Unity could be achieved by proselytism. Various speakers pleaded that respectable Christian communions should be dignified by the word 'Church' and treated as living and responsible entities in which the Word of God is preached and the sacraments administered. If there is to be dialogue, said Cardinal Léger of Montreal, it must be entered into by both sides with humility and love.

Two subjects of great importance came up in the course of the discussion. One was the question as to how far Roman Catholics could take part in joint services with Christians of other denominations. This had been a great problem and one which had caused a good deal of bitterness in the past. In spite of the 1949 Instructions, there had been occasions when, at the end of a public meeting in the Week of Prayer for Unity, the Roman Catholic members of the audience had walked out in a body rather than stay and say the Lord's Prayer together with their fellow believers. The excuse given was that if they prayed 'thy will be done' they would be praying for something quite different from the rest; but this was not very convincing. Now, in the Council, better sense prevailed. 'The widest possible latitude', said Bishop Flores Martin of Spain, 'should be allowed for participation in non-Catholic religious services in order to avoid the struggles which are all too common among those who should be living together in peace'; and Fr Capucci of the Basilians pleaded for more *communicatio in sacris*. 'The existence of such *communicatio* in cases where it was permitted was', he said, 'not a scandal. It was its absence that was scandalous'. Many indeed felt that regulations which prevented

Roman Catholics from even going inside a non-Roman church
– let alone attending an act of worship in one – ought to be
revised. Two years later the whole problem took an entirely
new turn when the Pope himself took part in a joint service in
Rome.[1]

The other problem which has done so much to bedevil relations between Rome and the rest of the Christian world has been
in the matter of mixed marriages. This question was not really
part of the Schema under discussion, but two speakers at least
referred to it as one of the obstacles to mutual respect and
charity. Cardinal Frings of Cologne was one of those who
mentioned it. He realised that mixed marriages did cause great
difficulty, and said that it would really be better if Catholics and
Protestants avoided falling in love with each other. Since this
was difficult to regulate, and since mixed marriages were, therefore, inevitable, he thought that the Church should declare that
marriages conducted by a non-Catholic minister were valid, and
should remove the penalties which were normally attached to
those concerned in them.

The point was also taken up by Bishop Ghattas, the Bishop
of Thebes-Luxor, who described conditions in Egypt. He told
the Council that it had always been the custom there for the
Roman part of the Church to recognise as valid marriages performed before a Coptic priest. But in 1949 this was stopped on
orders from Rome. He pointed out how disastrous this policy
had been, what unhappiness and even scandal it had created,
and he pleaded for a restoration of the conditions which had
existed before the Holy Office had stepped in.[2]

As the debate proceeded, it became increasingly clear that a
distinction would have to be made between relations with the
Orthodox Churches – so ancient, so holy, so Marian, so un-
reformed – and the Protestant Churches, some of which had, in
400 years, wandered so far from the traditions and practice of

[1] See above, pp. 30–31.   [2] *Council Speeches of Vatican II*, pp. 150–1.

the Catholic Church. But what about the Anglicans? Where did they come in?

It is, of course, probable that a good many of the fathers had never heard of them. Of the 2,300 bishops at the Council, over one quarter (600) came from Italy and Brazil where the opportunity of dialogue with Anglicans is fairly remote. But in northern Europe, the United States and the Commonwealth countries the bishops had had plenty of opportunity of meeting, and of finding out something about, their Anglican brethren. Many of them confessed that they found Anglicanism a baffling problem. They were amazed at the varieties of religious belief and of religious habits which could be found under one umbrella. They were shocked at the lack of discipline in some quarters, and confused by the readiness to surrender things which to them seemed of crucial importance for the sake of a patched-up union. Some of the missionary bishops with whom I discussed these things were apprehensive. One bishop from West Africa told me that, while he understood and admired Anglicans, Methodists and Presbyterians, he was amazed to find how ready they were to take part in joint services with the strangest of sects, some of whom were reviving pagan customs in the hopes of getting converts.

Those who had taken the trouble to find out something about Anglicanism realised that, in spite of its curious habits, it was obviously something quite different from other Protestant communities, and that it ought not, therefore, to be lumped together with them in the post-Reformation group. Bishop Collin of Digne in France was one of the first to call for special treatment for the Anglican Communion because it was in a special category of its own. This point was expanded by Archbishop Gouyon, coadjutor of Rennes, who said that in the Schema 'we look in vain for any clear allusion to the great Anglican communion, which in its origins is certainly quite distinct and different from the communities of the Reformation'. And again,

'It would satisfy me better if there were different and separate chapters for the Orthodox Churches, for the Anglican Communion, and for the communions which grew out of the Reformation.'[1] Later on Bishop Rupp of Monaco, a great Anglophile, said that in the Anglican Church we find many beautiful and inspiring things about bishops and their place in the Church, and he quoted Newman who, after twenty-one years in the Roman Catholic Church, said that 'for three centuries the Anglican Church had produced so many holy people, and accomplished so much good, that it could be explained only by a special intervention of Divine Providence' – an opinion which was expressed more recently by Fr Henry St John, O.P., who wrote: 'As I look back over the years I become more and more deeply convinced that in the providence of God the Church of England has a particular vocation, to bring together into organic unity the Catholicity of East and West and the Protestantism of Reformation Christendom.'[2] Meanwhile, Bishop Green of Port Elizabeth pleaded for a reconsideration at the highest level of the question of the validity of Anglican Orders.

While some of the French bishops were expressing their appreciation of the Anglican Church, the only speaker from England who had anything to say in favour of the Anglicans was Abbot Butler of Downside who thought it 'altogether appropriate' that there should be some special mention of the Anglican Church 'so wide-spread, so devoted to patristic antiquity, and which has deserved so well of the ecumenical movement.'

Only two of the English bishops were to be found among the 163 who took part in the debate on Ecumenism. One was Archbishop Heenan who started off by saying that 'the hierarchy of England and Wales gives its ready approval to the constitution *De Ecumenismo*, which it receives with joy'. But he then went on to say that he thought dialogue should take place only in the country of those taking part, presumably so that it could be

[1] *Ibid.*, pp. 115–17.   [2] *Blackfrairs*, January 1965.

under the control of the local hierarchy. In this he was supported by Archbishop Conway of Armagh, and, curiously
enough by Cardinal Bea. In some ways this seems a fair enough
proposal; but it was received with some apprehension by
Anglicans since so many of our most fruitful conversations have
been held outside England – in France, Belgium, Germany and
Italy. If such contacts were forbidden then a very serious blow
would be delivered to mutual understanding between our two
Churches.[1]

The other English prelate who took part in this debate was
Bishop Dwyer, then Bishop of Leeds. Living in a country in
which Roman Catholics are only a minority, he claimed to
know something about the 'separated brethren', and what he
had learnt of them did not fill him with much confidence for the
future. He referred, rather obliquely, to two recent publications
– Robinson's *Honest to God* and *A Quaker View on Sex* – neither of
which had brought him much comfort. It seemed to him that,
apart from the Roman Catholics, the Christians of England
were very uncertain as to where they stood both in regard to
faith and morals, some denying the Virgin Birth and the
Resurrection, some condoning conduct which the Christian
Church has always condemned. He warned the fathers of the
dangers of over-optimism. All was by no means rosy in the
Protestant garden.

In spite, however, of Bishop Dwyer's lucubrations, the Secretariat for Unity decided that something ought to be said in
favour of Anglicanism, and when they revised the Schema they
declared, while speaking of Churches which had separated
from Rome, that 'among those in which Catholic traditions and
institutions in part survive, the Anglican Communion stands
out' (*praeeminet*). Later this was changed to stating that the
Anglican Communion 'occupies a special place'. This, we were
told, was done so as not to offend the Old Catholics.

[1] For Heenan see *Council Speeches*, pp. 106–08, and for Bea, pp. 109–11.

The debate on chapters 1 – 3 lasted until 2 December. Cardinal Bea then announced that the two extra chapters – one on the Jews and one on Religious Liberty – would have to be left over until next year. This caused a good deal of disappointment, not least among American journalists who saw opportunities here of something more interesting than daily dispatches on dialogue, joint services, and such like. But it was clear that each of these chapters would need a good deal of time – the one on the Jews because of the inevitable opposition from bishops from the Arab countries, the one on Religious Liberty because it would raise some of the fundamental questions of human rights. In fact, the fathers had *two* years to wait before they were allowed to give their opinions on the rights of man.

The Schema on Ecumenism came back very much revised in 1964. The three chapters appeared as before, though the wording had been slightly altered. In its new form it appeared as:

1. Catholic Principles of Ecumenism (instead of Principles of Catholic Ecumenism, an obvious improvement).
2. The Practice of Ecumenism.
3. Churches and Ecclesial Communities separated from the See of Rome:
   (a) The Eastern Churches;
   (b) Separated Churches and Ecclesial Communities of the West.

These three chapters had been considerably improved as a result of the debate in the previous year. The Secretariat for Unity were determined to ignore the criticisms and adopt, so far as they could, the suggestions which had been made by the more progressive part in the Council. In spite of what Bishop Muldoon had said, they saw to it that a note of humility, and even of penitence, was sounded in accordance with the example set by the Holy Father himself. In fact, they take up his words and, after quoting from *I John* 1 : 10: 'If we say that we have no sin . . . his word is not in us,' they go on to say: 'In humble prayer we beg pardon of God and of our separated brethren just as we forgive them that trespass against us.' The new text also gives greater encouragement to corporate prayer, strongly commends dialogue on the basis of equality, demands a closer study of the beliefs and customs of the non-Roman Churches, and hopes for greater co-operation wherever possible.

By and large, the observers were pleased with the text in the form in which it was finally passed by large majorities. They were not so pleased when they discovered that, after the text had been debated more or less word by word, some higher authority – presumably the Pope – had made certain alterations. To those of us nourished on democratic and liberal principles this seemed outrageous; but then we didn't appreciate what it was like to have the Vicar of Christ as head of your Church. Most of the alterations were not of great significance, merely verbal changes to avoid ambiguity and obscurity. But there was one alteration which caused a good deal of dismay. In the text as passed by the Council there was a reference to the 'separated brethren' which said: 'Moved by the Holy Spirit, they *find* in the Sacred Scriptures God speaking to them in Christ' (§ 21). This was changed so as to read: 'While invoking the Holy Spirit they *seek* in these very Scriptures God as[1] he speaks to them in Christ'. To suggest that while you can seek God in the Scriptures you cannot be sure of finding him was distressing to Protestants, for whom the Bible holds a unique place. The first form of the sentence seemed so good; the later form so much less strong, so much less accurate. Some of the observers felt very strongly about this, one saying that it would take two generations to overcome this, and another remarking that the change had taken away much of the value of the whole Schema.[2] Of course there was the objection that, if you say

[1] There is some ambiguity here over the word '*quasi*' which can mean 'as' or 'as if'.

[2] Y. Congar, *Le Concile au jour le jour; Troisième Session* (Paris, 1965), p. 122.

that people can find God speaking to them in the Bible, you are throwing doubt on the right of the Church to interpret the Bible. There had, in fact, been a petition from some of the fathers to put the phrase in the sense of 'seeking' rather than of 'finding', but this had been rejected by the Secretariat and the Council had agreed. Why then change it at the last moment, knowing that such a change would inevitably distress those whom the Church was so anxious to please? Attempts have, of course, been made to justify the change[1]; but to us it looked as if the Pope had, in the end, been forced to give way to the more conservative element in his entourage.

The other alterations were not of much significance, and the text now stands more or less as it left the Council hall. On the whole, it is a good document from the point of view of those of us who are interested in making closer contacts with the Roman Church. It does not, of course, give a great deal of practical instruction, but that was not intended. The Decree was meant to lay down the principles on which the Church must act; it remains for the *Directorium* to go into greater detail, and for local hierarchies to apply the *Directorium*. But, in the meanwhile, doors have been opened. It is for all of us to see that they are never again closed.

[1] E.g. by Cardinal Jaegar in *A Stand on Ecumenism: The Council's Decree*, trans. Hilda Graef (London-Dublin, 1965), pp. 160-3.

CHAPTER FIVE

1964: *Hopes and Fears*

THOSE OF US WHO WATCHED TELEVISION ON THE evening of 6 January, 1964, saw what must have been one of the most interesting pictures ever shown on the screen. It was perhaps not very much to look at, just two elderly clergymen greeting each other; the significance lay in the fact that one of these elderly clergymen was Pope Paul VI and the other the Ecumenical Patriarch, Athenagoras I. The scene was Jerusalem to which each of them had gone, one from Rome and the other from Constantinople; and, although one might expect the heads of two great Christian Churches to be on friendly terms, it was in fact the first time that the holders of these two offices had met for many hundreds of years. For far away back in the eleventh century the Church of the East and the Church of the West had separated one from the other, and, although there had been attempts at reconciliation in 1274 and again in 1439, neither had really come to much and the schism had continued.

I took a personal interest in this encounter as I had, within recent months, met both of those taking part and had had talks about Christian unity with each. Each, I think, was genuinely anxious to meet the other, but so far all attempts to get them together had failed. The Patriarch told me that he had offered to go to Italy to meet Pope John and, to make things as easy as possible, had suggested that he should stay at the papal residence of Castel Gandolfo so that, after he had paid his visit to the Vatican, Pope John could have returned the call without going outside his own territory. But John had not accepted this proposal, and so no meeting had taken place. But now on neutral ground an encounter was possible. Perhaps not much was achieved by this. No doctrinal statement was issued; no concordat signed. But these were things which would come later. The important thing was that a barrier which had kept these two leaders apart for over 500 years had been broken and a real step towards Christian Unity had been taken.

During 1964 much thought was given by Christians of all denominations to what the Vatican Council was saying about Ecumenism. Though not yet promulgated, the decree was now pretty well known, and many questions were being asked. What, in fact, did this decree mean? What would it lead to? What was to be the relationship between the Roman Catholic Church and the World Council of Churches? What would happen if Rome decided to join the World Council of Churches on the ground that she could hardly be denied the right to belong to any organisation which describes itself as 'a fellowship of Churches which accept our Lord Jesus Christ as Lord and Saviour'? But would the World Council of Churches want Rome to join her? Would she swamp the whole thing just because of her vast bulk?

All these were difficult questions, made more difficult by the fact that, whereas up till now the World Council of Churches had been regarded as leading the movement towards Christian Unity, people were beginning to wonder whether the initiative was now falling into the hands of Rome. Rome had certainly totally changed her attitude towards the rest of the Christian world. Instead of saying 'the Catholic Church takes no part in ecumenical conferences or meetings',[1] she was now beginning to take a considerable part in the movement called 'Ecumen-

[1] See above, p. 92.

ical', and over against the progress and change which was
taking place at Rome the World Council at Geneva was beginning to look a little static. In view of this rapidly changing
situation, a writer could say that 'highly critical voices were
raised, both in Europe and in the United States, casting doubt
on the fitness of the World Council of Churches for a genuine
ecumenical reunion of Christians and advocating new negotiations, independent of the World Council of Churches, among
the Churches and with Rome. We cannot yet speak of a crisis in
the World Council of Churches', he continued, 'but there are
certainly signs of crisis which may be aggravated if Rome goes
on to further successes'.[1]

Early in 1964 the World Council decided that the time had
come to have a consultation between some of its leading
members and some of the official observers at the Vatican
Council. This consultation was held at Rummelsberg, near
Nuremburg, in July, 1964, and lasted four days. For us who had
been observers at the Council it was interesting to learn how the
World Council people were reacting to what was going on, and
I hope that the account of our experiences and impressions was
of value to them. Everyone, I think, was aware that the
Ecumenical Movement was moving into a totally new era, and
that the language and concepts of the past were really no longer
valid. It is, of course, very difficult for those who have given the
best part of their lives to ecumenical talk and administration
to make the necessary adjustments now that the ecumenical
movement has taken on new dimensions; but some adjustments
will have to be made. 'The Roman Catholic Church and the
World Council of Churches', wrote Dr Lukas Vischer, 'have a
vital interest in each other, and it is important that this fact of
belonging together in the ecumenical movement should find
some expression.'[2] It was to promote further dialogue that a

[1] *Herder Correspondence*, 1954, p. 283.
[2] *The Ecumenical Review*, xvi (1964), p. 392.

Joint Committee was set up in 1965 to arrange meetings at which the problems of Christian Unity, as it now appears, could be frankly discussed.[1]

The Rummelsberg discussions ended on 27 July, 1964, and ten days later Pope Paul issued *Ecclesiam Suam*, an encyclical letter addressed 'to the episcopate, the clergy, the faithful, and all men of good will', thus including in his appeal members of the non-Roman Churches. The letter proved to be disappointing not only to many of the 'men of goodwill' to whom it was partially addressed but also to a large number of the faithful, both clerical and lay. Language such as the following was not really calculated to help forward the cause of Christian Unity:

'Oh, it is neither pride', he said, 'nor presumption, nor obstinacy, nor folly, but a luminous certitude and our joyous conviction that we are indeed living members of the Body of Christ, that we are the authentic heirs of the Gospel of Christ, those who truly continue the work of the Apostles, that there dwells in us the great inheritance of truth and morality characterizing the Catholic Church, which today possesses intact the living heritage of the original, apostolic traditions.'[2]

Later, in discussing the dialogue with the 'separated brethren' he defends the doctrine of the primacy of Rome in these words:

'It distresses us to see how we, the promoter of such reconciliation, are regarded by many of the separated brethren as being its chief stumbling-block, because of the primacy of honour and jurisdiction which Christ bestowed upon the Apostle Peter, and which we have inherited from him. Do not some of them say that, if it were not for the primacy of the Pope, the reunion of the separated Churches with the Catholic Church would be easy?'[3]

to which the answer is: Yes, of course they do, because they can see so little justification for it in either history or theology.

[1] *Herder Correspondence*, 1965, pp. 200–01.
[2] *Ecclesiam Suam* (English version published by Tipografia Poliglotta Vaticana, 6 August 1964), pp. 33–4.
[3] *Ibid.*, p. 72.

From the point of view of ecumenism, *Ecclesiam suam* can hardly be regarded as a success. To many Protestants it looked as if the old 'triumphalism' was creeping back into the official statements of the Church. The tone with which Pope Paul had spoken at the opening of the Second Session in 1963 had been very different from this. The question now was what tone would he adopt when the Third Session opened on 14 September, 1964.

Again he spoke for some considerable time, mostly on the question of the place of the episcopate in the Church; but towards the end he turned to address the observers, once more expressing with great warmth his joy at having us there and pledging himself to continue the work for Unity. The most important passage was this:

> 'We shall strive, in loyalty to the unity of Christ's Church, to understand better and to welcome all that is genuine and admissible in the different Christian denominations that are distinct from us, and at the same time we beg of them to try to understand the Catholic faith and life better and, when we invite them to enter into the fulness of truth and charity which, as an unmerited blessing but also a formidable responsibility, Christ has charged us to preserve, we beg them not to take it in bad part, but as being prompted by respect and brotherly love. For that fulness of truth and charity will be made more manifest when all those who profess the name of Christ are reassembled into one.'[1]

Even though they might have some reservations about the phrase 'the fulness of truth and charity' into which members of non-Roman Churches were 'invited to enter', the opening speech of Pope Paul was, on the whole, well received by the observers. But many of them – as, indeed, many members of the Roman Catholic Church – were becoming increasingly anxious about what appeared to be a change of attitude and

[1] X. Rynne, *The Third Session*, p. 295. The whole address is here printed (pp. 287–95).

policy on the part of the Supreme Pontiff. 'In contrast to the spirit of joyous expectation', writes Xavier Rynne, 'that pervaded the world when Pope John XXIII announced the Council and brought its initial session to a successful close, the hopes of men seem to have been dampened by the more timorous and cautious Pauline spirit.'[1]

There was, in fact, much talk of the fact that the Pope appeared to be falling more and more under the influence of a small but strong group of curial officers of the most conservative kind. It would, indeed, take a very strong man to stand up to the pressures exerted upon him, for, whereas the more progressive and imaginative prelates were in Rome for only two or three months of the year, the Pope was subjected, for the other nine months, to the continual, daily influence of the Curia. It was they who decided what he should be told and what information should be kept from him; they who could visit him at any time and offer their advice; they whose job it was to advise him how to act in the innumerable decisions which he has to make.

There seems to be no doubt that this conservative and powerful group were busy impressing upon the Pope the fact that the Church was in great danger, that the ideas expressed in the Council by men like Suenens, Doepfner and Meyer were held by only a small minority, that it was the duty of the Pope to preserve the unity of the Church at all costs, that when the Council was over the Church would need a strong government, and so on. It must have been pressure such as this which induced the Pope to write in *Ecclesiam Suam*: 'If the term "reform" can be applied to this subject [i.e. the image of the Church] it is not to be understood in the sense of "change", but of a stronger determination to preserve the characteristic features which Christ impressed on the Church' – words which would be fair enough so long as one could be certain that these 'characteristic

[1] *Ibid.*, p. 2.

features' were impressed on the Church by Christ and not by people like Boniface VIII and Pius IX.

Looking back on the Third Session, when it was all over, Rynne could write: 'What the Third Session has revealed more clearly than ever before are the lengths to which Pope Paul is willing to go to soothe the feelings and assuage the doubts of this powerfully-placed group of resisters who, it is commonly believed, have no intention of accepting what they regard as virtual apostasy' (p. 6). And he concludes this passage with the words: 'What is perplexing and alarming is not that the Pope should feel he must conciliate the small group of officials whom he daily sees, but that he should be willing to risk making the mistake of Pius IX in 1870, in reverse, by appearing to sacrifice the majority to the minority' (p. 7).

It was perplexities and alarms such as this which brought the fathers back to Rome in 1964 with considerable reluctance. Many of them were worried as to what was going to happen. Many of them wondered whether the Council was really going to succeed in its dual task of *aggiornamento* and *ecumenismo*.

The First Session had been fun. It was all so new and exciting. There was John XXIII, the Pope who had won the love and affection of the whole world, the man who had shattered the image of the papacy – so carefully built up by Pius XII – as cold, tyrannical and aloof. It was John who had had the audacity, without consulting anyone, to call a Council. Well, let's see what we can make of it. It was fun having a crack at the Curia, fun throwing out the Schemata so that the old men had to do their homework all over again, fun listening to Liénart and Maximos IV, fun meeting all these bishops from all over the world, fun chatting in the Bar-Jonah, picking up the latest stories about Ottaviani and Cushing.

The Second Session had also had its points. It was nice seeing old friends again after nine months' absence. It was interesting to see how the Council would get on under new management. It was good getting down to a big subject like Collegiality, especially as it could do so much to boost the ego of every bishop in the world. It was fine, too, to see the old Church beginning to take an interest in Ecumenism. After all, other Christian folk were arguing about unity; why shouldn't we plunge into the fray? Yes, there was much to be said for 1963.

But by 1964 the fun was beginning to wear off. There were no new experiences to look forward to. It was going to be the same grind all over again. Another three months away from the diocese. . . . How much longer can we expect our people to put up with this? And look at the programme. *Fourteen* Schemata to read, and all the amendments and modi that go with them. So when Pope Paul had said to the fathers in December, 1963, 'we must once again bid each other farewell and go our separate ways after these happy days of momentous brotherly conference', he sounded a bit like a headmaster telling the boys that he knew how much they would miss all the joys of school life when they got home for the holidays.

There were, I believe, a good many doubts and fears lurking in the minds of many of the Council fathers when they returned to Rome for the Third Session. And among these was some uncertainty as to what Pope Paul was going to do. No one doubted his integrity, nor indeed his desire to promote reform and renewal of the Church; what they doubted was his ability to stand up to this organised bullying to which he was daily subjected. Many of us felt that there was a certain hardening process going on. The Council was being more and more divided between those who were determined to make it a great opportunity for progress and those who were prepared to do their utmost to prevent this. I know that not all the Council fathers felt this. Archbishop Heenan, for example, said in Rome on 18 September: 'Nobody within the Council now talks about conservatives and progressives. These were always rather inappropriate labels, but now they look merely foolish'[1]; but, in the observers' box, and among the bishops to whom I spoke, just the opposite seemed to be true. Many felt that there was a very real division among the fathers, a deep feeling that two big forces were coming to grips and that this was not just a clash of opinions but of policies and even of moralities.

The events of the Third Session bore this out. Twice the Council was really angry, more angry that I ever saw it, and both times over a very controversial but essential document – on Religious Liberty. On the first occasion when this happened, feeling ran so high that seventeen cardinals felt that they must make an appeal direct to the Pope to prevent what they believed to be a grave miscarriage of justice, beginning their letter with the phrase: *magno cum dolore*. Xavier Rynne thought the Third Session 'the most disappointing of all'. 'Why,' he asks, 'did so many Fathers leave Rome in a state of sadness and bewilderment? Why did the phrase "*magno cum dolore*" – the opening words of an urgent petition to the Pope at a moment of crisis – become a kind of catchword for the whole session? Why did a session that began with such promise end in such gloom?'[2]

The first business to which the Council had to turn, after the opening ceremonies, was the last two chapters of the big Constitution on the Church, one dealing with the eschatological nature of the Church and the other with the Blessed Virgin Mary.[3] Having spent four mornings on these they were able to turn to the first of a group of five Schemata all of which dealt in some way with the Church's ministry.

The first of these was called 'The Pastoral Office of Bishops in the Church' and had been written to replace a previous document which, after a rather acrimonious debate, had been rejected in the previous November.[4] This new document was

---

[1] *English Bishops at the Council: Third Session*, p. 138.
[2] *The Third Session*, p. 2.   [3] See above, pp. 74–7.   [4] See above, p. 87.

meant to be a practical and pastoral appendix to the more theological statement about collegiality and the place of bishops in the Church which had now been accepted for publication.

No one can become a bishop without discovering that he has a dual rôle to perform – that of being a father-in-God to his people and that of being a leader in the Church. Anglican bishops in England find that they are expected to 'give a lead' in all kinds of social and political matters, many of which are beyond their ken and for which they have neither training nor inclination. This is increased by the fact that the bishops have long been members of the House of Lords and, therefore, required to play some part in the government of the country. Modern Roman Catholic bishops do not have to carry this particular burden; but nonetheless, because of their position, they are expected to be ready to express their views on a number of subjects of public interest, to take their part in the government of the Church, to study and support the work of the Church throughout the world, to have at least some idea of what is going on in the world of scholarship, to raise vast sums of money for all sorts of projects, and, on top of this, to be at the beck and call of their clergy and their laity. All this makes a bishop's life a very full one; but, fundamentally, most bishops are more concerned with looking after their flocks than they are with the job of contributing to the work of the Church as a whole. This new Schema was, therefore, an attempt to describe the *pastoral* office of a bishop and, as such, it appealed to the vast majority of the prelates.

After some preliminary remarks intended to link this Schema up with the relevant passages of *De Ecclesia*, and a few cracks at the Curia, demanding a reorganisation of 'these departments which have furnished distinguished assistance to the Roman Pontiff', the decree gets on to the work of a bishop in his diocese as teacher, sanctifier and governor. The picture which emerges is that of a good shepherd who knows and loves his flock, does his best to see that the needs of the faithful are adequately met, and encourages the Church to go out and win souls for Christ. All are included, for the Schema goes so far as to say that he should deal lovingly with the separated brethren and the gypsies. The latter part deals with more practical matters such as the size of dioceses, the work of auxiliary and coadjutor bishops, diocesan officials, synods, councils and conferences.

Only three days were allowed for the discussion of this document, and nothing of very great importance was said. Although a few wanted more emphasis on the authority of a bishop in ruling his flock, the majority preferred the pastoral approach as being far more in keeping with what the present day demanded.

Later in the session the fathers were presented with a document on the life and ministry of a priest. This, like the Schema on the bishops, was intended to follow on what had been said about the priesthood in *De Ecclesia*, and was therefore reduced to a series of ten propositions covering only three pages of print in the fascicule which was distributed. As soon as they saw this many of the bishops felt unhappy about it. After all that had been said about bishops, both in *De Ecclesia* and in the Schema on their pastoral work, they considered this flimsy and rather superficial document totally unworthy. Since the Constitution on the Church had already said something (though surprisingly little) about the priesthood, the commission which drew up this Schema contented themselves with some practical considerations about what priests should wear (and not wear), about learning a little sociology and psychology, about moving from one diocese to another, about salaries and things of that kind. This was all very well; but, as was pointed out, it failed altogether to do justice to the subject. Several speakers pointed out that it gave no kind of inspiration to the priests, and one bishop from Brazil (where there are few enough priests anyhow) called it an 'insult'. Some drew attention to the fact that it was asking

priests to accept far more discipline than the bishops were prepared to put upon themselves; others said it served only to
'downgrade' the priests and make them feel that they were
just the playthings of the bishops.

It was not long, therefore, before it became quite clear that
this Schema would not do, and on the second day of the discussion it was rejected and sent back to the commission to be
rewritten.

The third Schema which dealt with the ministry was one on
'Priestly Formation' or the training of men for the ministry.
This also appeared in the form of a series of propositions, but
unlike the Schema on the priesthood it got a fairly good recep-
tion. It began well, for its first statement was that the way in
which men were trained for the priesthood must vary from
place to place and be decided by the local hierarchy. This was
very popular, as many bishops felt that they wanted to decide
how their men should be trained and not be forced to conform
to a pattern laid down by the Congregation of Seminaries,
Universities and Studies in Rome under the presidency of the
aged, but still active, Cardinal Pizzardo. Archbishop Garonne
of Toulouse was among the most outspoken in his criticisms of
the Congregation and in his demands for a new central office
made up of representatives from all over the world, and was
rewarded for his pains by being subsequently appointed as pro-
prefect of the Congregation, the first time, it was said, that a
bishop from outside Italy had been summoned to take charge of
one of the big offices in Rome. Others from outside the Council
also applauded this move for local direction of studies, among
them Fr Congar, O.P., who said that, having taught in a
seminary for twenty-three years, he knew something of the 'in-
conveniences' (to put it politely) which he had had to endure
from a Congregation in Rome which was known to be among
the least progressive.[1]

[1] Y. Congar, *Le Concile au jour le jour: Troisième Session* (Paris, 1965), p. 110.

Having given themselves the right to draw up their own courses of study, the bishops went on to consider what sort of training they would wish to have in these days. In the course of the debate four points came up for discussion.

First, there was the question of minor or junior seminaries. At what age should a boy be removed from his fellows and put into the pipe-line out of which he would eventually emerge as a priest? In many countries it has long been the custom to do this when the child reaches the age of eleven. Angelo Roncalli entered the minor seminary at Bergamo at that age, and from that time onwards everything he did was organised in preparation for his ultimate ordination. Those who have read his *Journal of a Soul* will realise what this meant. His whole life was mapped out for him, everything he did was done under the watchful eye of his director, any possibility of his coming into contact with 'the world' was carefully removed. As a result he could write in his diary: 'I will never, never meddle in matters concerning newspapers, bishops, topics of the day'; and, when on holiday: 'I tend to linger too long in the kitchen after supper, talking things over with my family.'[1] Was this sort of thing healthy? Did we want, as spiritual guides today, men who knew so little of the world or of how ordinary people lived? Was there a danger of boys being 'trapped' by this system? If, from the age of eleven, it had been taken for granted he was to be a priest, would it not take great courage, after ten years or so of free education, for a young man to say that he did not feel a vocation to the priesthood? Was the system, perhaps, responsible for some of the subsequent failures in the priesthood?

The second point was a similar one, and raised the question as to whether it would not be advisable to send ordinands to the ordinary universities. At present the majority of men studying for the priesthood spend their last years at a Catholic University or College where, again, they are cut off from normal contact

[1] John XXIII, *Journal of a Soul*, trans. Dorothy White, pp. 39, 41.

with their contemporaries. The Anglican Church has never adopted this plan and sends its ordinands to places of higher education where they will rub shoulders not only with Christians of other denominations but with humanists, agnostics, atheists and everything else. This, we feel, is good for them. It helps them to understand something about the world in which their ministry will have to be fulfilled, and it teaches them how to defend the faith that is in them. But it is not so with the Roman Catholic ordinand who, normally, has passed from a Catholic primary school to a Catholic secondary school and so to a Catholic university or college where he has very little opportunity of finding out what other people think or of sharpening his own weapons in the face of criticism and disagreement. The Schema on Priestly Formation talks about the student learning how to meet the unbeliever; but how is he to do this? Out of text-books? or from lectures delivered by men who have themselves had very little contact with the world? Many of the bishops saw clearly the obvious weaknesses in the present system, but others feared that if the young men were allowed to see too much of the world they might be lost to the ministry.

The third point concerned the place of mediaeval scholasticism, and especially of the works of Thomas Aquinas, in the curriculum of a modern seminary. In the discussion of this subject we saw more clearly than anywhere the division of opinion between those who could not imagine how anyone could be prepared for the priesthood without a very stiff dose of Thomism, and those who thought that some rather more modern ideas might well be considered. Cardinal Léger was surely right in saying that, while Aquinas should be studied because of his 'scientific and spiritual approach' to knowledge, we must not nowadays be too much tied down by what he actually said. The cardinal criticised the use of the phrase 'perennial philosophy' in the Schema, as if the conclusions of thirteenth-century Scholasticism of one particular school were infallible and irreformable, and he wanted the door left open to more modern types of thought. Cardinal Léger got some support from other liberal thinkers, but his suggestion that S. Thomas was not the only philosopher worth consideration roused a storm of protest from some of the more conservative prelates who could not visualise any course of study which did not make the *Summa Theologica* the basis of all that was taught. But the fulminations of Ruffini, Bacci, Staffa and others were not taken too seriously by some of the younger bishops who amused themselves by suggesting that, at the end of the Council, the bishops should join hands and sing:

'Should auld Aquinas be forgot.'

The fourth point was concerned with the training of a priest for pastoral work in the world of today. Cardinal Suenens criticised the seminaries as being pale imitations of the religious houses and scarcely aware of the problems of modern man. He wanted much more practical training, especially in preaching and spiritual direction. In this he was supported by Bishop Schmitt of Metz who said that the cultural background of the older seminaries was the world of the Middle Ages. He thought a lot of *aggiornamento* was needed here if men were to be trained to deal with the problems of the jet age. Escuin the coadjutor bishop of Malaga in Spain suggested that a man should not be ordained priest until he had spent two years 'in active pastoral experience' – a suggestion of some interest to the Anglican observers, since our men normally spend the year of their diaconate in parochial work.

After three days of debate the fathers decided, by a very large majority, that they approved in general of this Schema, and it was sent back to the commission for final amendment. When it came back in the following year it showed that the commission had taken due note of what had been said. Attempts were made to ensure that no man was ordained against his will, that the pastoral needs of the ministry were duly considered in all seminary training, that, so far as possible, the student should learn how to face the unbeliever and critic, that he should be taught something about the 'non-catholic' Churches so as to enter into the ecumenical movement, that arrangements were made for post-ordination teaching, and so on. One of the more encouraging features of this decree, from our point of view, is the insistence upon closer study of the Scriptures, for it is in the field of biblical knowledge that we feel that the Roman Church is so often deficient. I remember the surprise and admiration which I evoked from a large group of seminarians in Rome when I told them something of our programme of biblical study, and pointed out that any Anglican priest who says his daily offices regularly reads practically the whole of the Old Testament once, and the New Testament twice, in the course of each year.

The discussion on training for the priesthood was naturally followed with considerable interest by the observers, a good many of whom had been concerned, at some time or other in their lives, with the task of preparing men for the ministry. The next subject, that of the Religious Orders was, on the other hand, unfamiliar to most of them. There were, however, in the tribune of S. Longinus at least four men who were members of religious orders – the two brothers from Taizé, Fr Ernest John of the Brotherhood of the Ascension in Delhi and Br Wilhelm Schmidt of the Evangelische Michaelsbruderschaft in Germany.

The religious orders are one of the great glories of the Roman Catholic Church, and many of us deeply regret that, in the sixteenth century and for the worst possible reasons, all the religious houses in England were suppressed and the whole idea of the religious life banished from the land. It is only recently that this essential element in the life of the Church has crept back, but it is slowly expanding, and there are said to be more Anglican nuns in England today than there were nuns here in

the year 1500. In the Church of Rome the members of the
religious orders play a very large part in the work of the
Church, many bishops having more regular than secular
priests among their clergy. In education, in medical work, in
the mission field, in every kind of social activity, the work of
the religious is of the utmost importance, while, in the background, are the contemplatives supporting with their prayers
the more practical work of the Church. The religious orders are,
therefore, something of which the Roman Catholic Church has
every reason to be proud. Would that other Churches were able
to attract such large numbers of men and women to a life of
such dedication and devotion.

But, like every other institution, the religious orders are
always in need of reform, and a Council could hardly fail to try
to do something to make them more devout, more efficient, a
sharper tool in the hands of the Church. The conditions in
which religious had to do their work were changing rapidly;
the question was whether they themselves were keeping pace
with the changes, and whether such changes as they were
undergoing were the right ones. For there was known to be a
certain amount of criticism of the religious and of their way of
life. Traditionally, they were the most committed, the most self-
sacrificing, the ones who had really taken seriously and literally
the evangelical counsels of poverty, chastity and obedience, the
men and women who had forsaken all for Christ. But was this
the image which they presented to the world today? Did the
vow of poverty mean that their life was harder than that of their
fellows? People wondered about this when they saw some of
their new monasteries, their cars, the fact that there was always
money available to go to the other end of the world to take
part in some conference. Did the vow of obedience make life
much more difficult than that of the secular priest, or layman,
living according to a rigid self-discipline which was necessary if
he was to fulfil his ministry and vocation? Did the vow of

chastity mean much more than what was expected of all priests and what was the lot of a good many women?

A whole chapter of *De Ecclesia* had extolled the religious orders as the most dedicated and sanctified members of the Church, as being 'involved in the service and honour of God on a new and special warrant', of having adopted 'the way of life which the Son of God took up on his entry into the world to do the Father's will', and so on. The problem now was to see that the religious orders carried out the necessary reforms to make them worthy of such praise.

The Schema offered to the Council was in the form of nineteen propositions. The whole thing was very short, occupying only four pages of print, though it had been reduced from a very much longer document of nearly 100 pages. In its truncated form it was felt to be too slight to be of much good. As Cardinal Bea, himself a monk, said: 'There is something of a crisis in religious life', and a crisis of this magnitude is not going to be solved by a few platitudes. In fact, the subject was big enough to demand more thorough treatment, and this is what the Council eventually agreed must be done. It took only a couple of days to make it clear to the fathers that some pretty drastic revision was necessary, and on 12 November the Schema went down for redrafting.

When it came back the following year it had been changed from nineteen propositions 'On religious' to a conciliar decree on 'The Adaptation and Renewal of the Religious Life'. This was far more worthy of so big a subject and was received with gratitude by the fathers.

The last document which dealt with the ministry was that on the 'Missionary Activity of the Church', another big subject which demanded imaginative and constructive thought. Pope Paul, having always declared himself to be greatly interested in this subject, appeared himself in the *aula* on the day when the document on Missions was to be presented, and made a speech

extolling the draft which was to be discussed. This was an unprecedented event, and was marked by having one of the
Eastern liturgies, on this occasion an Ethiopian rite. We had
had this in the previous year and knew it to be something rich
and strange. Like all Eastern rites it is a 'dialogue Mass' and
demands a choir; so some students from the Ethiopian College
had come along to make the thing go. They had brought with
them various instruments – drums, cymbals, castanets – with
which to accompany their rather doleful singing, and when the
liturgy was over they thought the Holy Father would like to see
what they could do. So they went and sat on the floor in front
of the presidents' table and gave of their best. Frantic secretaries rushed about, waving their arms in gestures of despair,
but Pope Paul seemed to be enjoying the entertainment provided. After all, he doesn't often get a chance of enjoying
himself.

When eventually the black boys had been removed, the Pope
made his speech in which he said that, although some amendments might be necessary, he hoped the Council would accept
the draft which was now to be laid before it. He then left
Cardinal Agagianian to present the Schema and retired to the
papal apartments.

This Schema, like the others, was very short and written in
the form of thirteen propositions. It began well by saying that
there must be proper collaboration between the bishops and the
heads of the religious orders. This was a subject on which many
of the bishops felt strongly. The religious orders were potentially
a source of great strength to them; but, in fact, the bishops often
found that they could not get the help they wanted as the
monks and nuns were under orders from Rome or some other
centre. One bishop in Africa told me that he had a nunnery in
his diocese containing 150 sisters, but only ten of them were
allowed to help him in the work of the diocese; and the debate
on the religious orders had produced similar evidence from

other places. After this, the Schema went on to explain that 'mission' was something in which the whole Church was involved, not just those working in the 'mission-field' nor, indeed only those who were members of the Roman Catholic Church, for the Schema demanded 'co-operation in social and technical matters, as well as in matters of culture *and religion* with non-catholic Christians', as well as saying that all men and women in training for missionary work should be taught something about the work of other Christian bodies and about the problems and fruits of ecumenism. This was particularly appropriate, as a few weeks previously, when the Pope was canonizing some of the Uganda martyrs, special reference was made to the Anglicans who had suffered with them, and the Anglican archbishop in Uganda had been flown to Rome at the Pope's expense to take part in the ceremonies.

But, in spite of much that was good in the Schema, the fathers again thought it unworthy and inadequate. It was attacked on the grounds that it was patronising to the missionary provinces, that it was old-fashioned in asking the wealthier parts of the Church to pray and pay for the missionaries, that it failed to give any conception of the greatness of the task which lay before the Church. 'There is here only frustration', said Bishop Lamont of Umtali in Rhodesia, 'no fire, no inspiration, just a few dry and miserable propositions'. Many agreed with him, and on the third day of the debate it was decided by 1,601 votes to 311, to ask for it to be revised.

There is no place where co-operation between the Christian Churches is more urgent than in the mission-field. The task of evangelism is so great that we cannot afford to play little games to try to score off each other. There has been far too much of this in the past, far too much energy wasted in converting Catholics to Protestantism and Protestants to Catholicism. Naturally it is easier to win over a slightly disgruntled or ambitious member of a Christian Church than to convert a

E

Moslem or a Hindu to the Faith. But the fact that the success of
a mission has often been measured by the number of its converts has led to proselytism and rivalry for which the Church
will one day have to answer.

No one wishes to accuse the Roman Church of indulging in
this form of 'one-upmanship' any more than any other Christian
community; but we were delighted to see, in the final form of
the decree on Missions, four new and important statements.
These are as follows:

(1) In so far as religious conditions allow, ecumenical activity
should be furthered in such a way that, excluding any appear-
ance of indifference or confusion on the one hand, or of un-
healthy rivalry on the other, Catholics should co-operate in a
brotherly spirit with their separated brethren, according to
the norms of the Decree on Ecumenism. . . . This co-operation
should be undertaken not only among private persons, but
also, subject to approval by the local Ordinary, among church
or ecclesial communities and their works.

(2) If perchance in certain regions, groups of men are to be found
who are kept away from embracing the Catholic Faith because they cannot adapt themselves to the peculiar form which
the Church has taken on there, it is hoped that this condition
will be provided for in a special way, until such times as all
Christians can gather together in one community.

(3) In co-ordination with the Secretariat for Promoting Christian
Unity, let it [i.e the Office for the Propagation of the Faith]
search out ways and means for bringing about and directing
fraternal co-operation as well as harmonious living with
missionary undertaking of other Christian communities, that
as far as possible the scandal of division may be removed.

(4) [After reminding Christians that they are 'the light of the
world and the salt of the earth'] . . . This testimony of good
life will more easily have its effect if it is given in unison with
other Christian communities, according to the norms of the
Decree of Ecumenism.

There was a fifth passage urging those in the mission-field to
work together with other baptised Christians so far as was

possible and 'if they are not yet able to give a clear witness to one Faith they should at least treat each other with respect and love'; but this was struck out of the final text for reasons which are by no means clear. Many of us were sorry that a call to mutual 'respect and love' should have to be omitted; but, even without this, the final form of the decree on the Church's Missionary Activity gives great hope for fuller co-operation in a field where Christians cannot afford to quarrel.

It will be remembered that in 1963, after the Schema on Ecumenism had been presented to the Council, two further chapters were added, one on the Jews and the other on Religious Liberty. In view of the shortage of time, however, these two chapters were not debated, though a promise was made that they would definitely be on the agenda for 1964.

Chapter 4 of the decree on Ecumenism was entitled: 'On the attitude of Catholics towards non-Christians, and especially the Jews'. It was very short, but there was a feeling that something ought to be said about the nation out of which Christianity sprang. Ecumenism was bound up with the history of salvation; but the history of salvation could not be understood without going right back to the call of Abraham and the formation of the Chosen People. Moreover, everyone knew that the Jews had fared very badly at the hands of the Christian Church in the past, and there had been some very nasty scenes in Rome itself in days gone by. In addition to all this there had been rumours that Pius XII had failed to do all that he might have done to save the Jews from extermination in Germany, rumours which had been encouraged by Rolf Hochhuth's recent play, *The Representative*. The image of the Church in its attitude towards the Jews was, therefore, not very good; and many thought that the time had come to clear things up a bit. Hence this short statement declaring that the Jews were 'beloved for their fathers' sake' (*Romans* 11 : 28) and should, there-

fore, no longer be described as 'deicides' or 'the cursed people'.
Anti-semitism was a very horrid thing, and Christians must be
careful not to allow it to fester in society.

All this was well meant and seemed harmless enough. But
when the draft came up again in 1964 – still as part of *De
Ecumenismo* – certain changes had been made. The text repeated
the biblical ideas about the common inheritance shared by
Christians and Jews, but this time it quoted another verse from
Romans expressing the Christian hope that, in the fullness of
time, 'all Israel shall be saved' (*Romans* 11 : 26). It left out the
word 'deicide' altogether, and contented itself with saying that
Christians must not suggest that modern Jews can, in any way,
be held responsible for the death of Christ.

All this seemed fairly innocuous, but it immediately caused
an uproar. The Jews asserted that the Church had gone anti-
semitic, that the phrase about all Israel being saved was rank
proselytism, that the removal of the phrase forbidding the use
of the word 'deicide' meant that Christians could, after all,
accuse the Jews of killing Christ, and so on. Then, on top of all
this, there was a growing political protest from the Arab countries, who took these modest and charitable statements as an
attempt to support the state of Israel. The Council was, therefore, faced with a war on two fronts. On one side was world
Jewry (which is very strong in America) condemning the draft
as anti-semitic, while, on the other side, were the Arab states
(which contain a considerable number of patriarchs and
bishops) declaring that the draft was Zionist and pro-Israel.

Cardinal Bea had the difficult task of presenting the new chapter, which he did in the most loving and irenic way. He urged the
fathers to treat this as a purely religious question, a desire to
show love and goodwill towards a people who had suffered much
in the past, and nothing whatever to do with middle-east politics,
Zionism, the Union of Arabic Republics or anything else.

The debate brought no less than thirty-four speakers to the

microphone, many of them anxious to lay once for all the ghost of anti-semitism in the Roman Catholic Church. Most of them admitted that they thought the earlier statement more tactful, but all of them were anxious to do something towards putting to right what had been a great wrong. Not so Cardinal Ruffini of Palermo, who had swallowed wholesale the views put out in a recently published booklet accusing the Jews and the Free-masons of engineering a mighty plot to overthrow the Church, and who now proceeded to pass on these accusations to the Council. It took a host of cardinals, including Lercaro, Léger, Cushing, König, Meyer and Ritter, to calm things down and encourage the fathers to make a gesture of goodwill to an oft-persecuted people. But there was still considerable opposition from the Arab countries as well as some justifiable criticism from East of Suez that, although the document claims to deal with the non-Christian world, nothing whatever was said about Hindus, Shintos, Buddhists, Confucians and the rest.

In its final form the draft tried to incorporate the points which had been made in the debate. More attention was given to the other non-Christian religions, which had hitherto been curiously overlooked, and a further attempt to satisfy the Jews was made by stating as a historical fact that 'the Jewish author-ities, and those who followed their lead, pressed for the death of Christ', without suggesting that anyone was particularly to blame. It also denounced all persecution, all anti-semitism, and all racial discrimination.

But, even with these improvements, the statement which is now called a 'Declaration on the Relation of the Church to non-Christian Religions', remains a rather feeble document. The fact is that you can't deal adequately with world religions in 1,500 words, especially when 600 of these words are devoted to the Jews only; and it was perhaps inevitable that distinguished members of some of these religions should have felt that the Council would have been wiser to have left the subject alone if they couldn't do the job a little better. Nor was the document at all popular with the Jews, who found it patronising, condescending, unsympathetic. Perhaps, however, in the circumstances, it was the best thing that could have been achieved in the face of so much opposition and misunderstanding.

The other additional chapter to the decree on Ecumenism dealt with the subject of Religious Liberty. This had first come out in 1963; but, in view of the shortage of time, it had been held over to the following year. 'Quod defertur non aufertur' ('what is put off is not put away'), Bea had said; so everyone was much interested in the document which was placed before the Council on 23 September, 1964.

Bishop de Smedt of Bruges introduced it on behalf of the Secretariat for Unity which had drawn it up on the basis of the 380 written observations which the fathers had sent in during the nine-months' recess. The bishop pointed out that Religious Liberty was something very much more than tolerance which is a negative thing, the agreement not to take action against those whose views are different from your own. The foundation of Religious Liberty is the nature of man as created by God, and it is concerned with human dignity and with a man's right to obey his conscience even though you may think it is leading him astray. Naturally it is man's duty to inform his conscience by a study of divine law and the teaching of the Church; but, if any man has done this with sincerity, then he must be free to believe and to do what he thinks is right, so long as he does not threaten public order or the rights and liberties of other people.

This principle is, of course, vital to any kind of ecumenical co-operation and dialogue, as the draft statement makes clear. Not only does it state this fact, but it goes on to declare that every man has the right to practise his religion not only privately but publicly, and that those who believe with him have the right to function as a religious assembly or community even in the heart of a country which is predominantly Roman Catholic.

The Church must, of course, proclaim the truth as she has received it; but it is her duty always to deal charitably, prudently and patiently with those whom she believes to be in error, giving them freedom of expression while doing all she can to help them to see the truth.

In her efforts to bring men to the 'true faith', she must never use any kind of force or undue persuasion. No one must be made to renounce his faith unless he does so freely and willingly. This freedom of religion applies not only to non-Roman Christians but to all men of any faith or of no faith. The Catholic Church, says the draft decree, vindicates the true and proper right of every person to observe and give witness to his private and public duties towards God and man. This right can be limited only if his behaviour can be regarded as gravely contrary to the very purpose of human and civilised society.

Finally the draft deals with the other side of the picture and declares that governments must not impose upon their subjects the profession or rejection of any religion whatsoever, nor must they put any restraint on any person for purely religious reasons. Moreover, this principle must apply not only to individuals but also to groups who must have the right to proclaim what they believe, though not to proselytise.

This liberal statement was naturally welcomed by the observers who saw here a real change from the old intransigence of the past. This year was the centenary of the publication of the *Syllabus of Errors* by Pius IX in 1864, in which the Pope had denounced as pernicious such beliefs as these: 'that every man is free to embrace and profess the religion he shall believe to be true', 'that eternal salvation may (at least) be hoped for of all those who are not in the true Church of Christ', 'that the Church has not the power of availing herself of force, or of any direct or indirect temporal power' – and so on, *ad nauseam*.[1] That exactly

---

[1] Denzinger *Enchiridion*, Nos. 1715, 1717, 1724, etc.: cf. H. Bettenson, *Documents of the Christian Church*, p. 380.

one hundred years later the Church should be proposing the exact opposite of all this was something which the observers (and many others) found most interesting and encouraging.

It will be clear, from the summary of the Schema, that it was really concerned with two quite different things – one the right of religious minorities to exist and to function freely even in communities which are largely of another type of Christian religion; the other the right of the Christian Church, of whatever denomination, to carry on its work in an atheistic or hostile state. So far as the second of these is concerned there was, of course, no difference of opinion; but on the first of them the Council was sharply divided.

How, many of the fathers were asking, can anyone believe that it is right to allow Protestants to go about teaching error? Would not this decree encourage 'indifferentism' and confusion, the popular belief that we are all going to the same place and that one route is as good as another? What we want, said Cardinal Ruffini, is a declaration on 'tolerance', not on 'liberty', for error has no rights; and the Cardinal Archbishop of Santiago lamented the fact that the text appeared to be solemnly confirming the Liberalism which the Church had so often condemned. But the fears and apprehensions of men of this school were quickly drowned in a series of excellent speeches from Cardinals Léger, Cushing, Meyer and Ritter, all of whom supported the Schema wholeheartedly. It was then left to Cardinal Ottaviani to back up the conservative cause, which he did by declaring that 'it is illegal to admit freedom to propagate a religion when this may threaten the unity of a Catholic nation', and by referring to the various concordats whereby the Papacy had come to terms with governments in different parts of the world. Cardinal Michael Browne (known to the more frivolous prelates as 'Caveamus Browne' since he was always pleading for caution) said that the present text was wholly unacceptable since it gave equal rights to error and truth.

The conservative line got some support from the bishops. Archbishop Parente, one of Ottaviani's colleagues as Assessor of the Holy Office, said that the text could not be accepted since it put the rights of man before the rights of God; Archbishop Nicodemo of Bari piously declared that error can have no rights; and the Bishop of Campos in Brazil remarked that the public profession of religion should be allowed only to members of the 'true faith'. But there was a great deal of support from the other side, especially from the American bishops who were particularly sensitive to the accusation that the Roman Catholic Church believes in religious liberty only when it is in a minority. Others, including Colombo, the Pope's personal theologian (? and mouthpiece), said: 'Unless we have this declaration, there can be no dialogue with men of goodwill.'

Many bishops were anxious to speak on this issue, which, from the point of view of the Church's image, was one of the most important subjects to come before the Council; but, after two days of discussion, it was decided to close the debate at this stage and let the Secretariat for Unity get on with the revision of the text. By this time it was fairly clear that the majority of the fathers was in favour of the Schema, but that there was a small and determined minority which was going to do its best to wreck the whole thing.

Everyone now thought that the text was safely in the hands of Cardinal Bea and the Secretariat for Unity which had produced it and would be responsible for it until it reached its final form. But they had not allowed for the intriguing powers of the minority, which counted among its members Cardinal Cicognani, the chairman of the central co-ordinating committee, and Archbishop Felici, the general secretary of the Council. These two, without consulting other members of the Central Commission, took it upon themselves to declare that the Pope wished the matter to be handled, not by the Secretariat for Unity, but by a new mixed commission which would include people like 'Caveamus' Browne and such arch-conservatives as Lefebvre, the Superior General of the Holy Ghost Fathers, and Fernandez, the Master General of the Dominicans. But, when Cardinal Bea asked whether it was indeed true that the Pope had said this, Felici was forced to admit that he had not, though he felt sure it was what the Pope would wish to happen.

As soon as they realised what was going on behind the scenes, a group of seventeen cardinals met together and drew up a letter to the Pope which began thus:

> 'Holy Father,
> 'With great sorrow (*Magno cum dolore*) we have learned that the declaration on religious liberty, although in accord with the desire of the great majority of the Fathers, is to be entrusted to a certain mixed committee . . . three of whom appear to be opposed to the general feelings of the Council on this matter. This news is for us a source of extreme anxiety and very disquieting.'

They went on to say:

> 'Impelled by this anxiety, we ask Your Holiness with great insistence that the declaration be returned to the normal procedure of the Council and dealt with according to the existing rules, so that there may not result from it great evils for the whole People of God.'[1]

The Pope acted quickly. He immediately gave orders that the Schema was to be safely left in the hands of the Secretariat for Unity, though he would allow a mixed committee to examine it before it was finally placed before the Council.

This incident left a very unpleasant taste in the mouth. As I have said above, the fathers were beginning to realise that the Council was revealing, not just a clash of opinions but of moralities.[2]

It was now early October and the Council was due to end on

[1] The Text will be found in Rynne, *The Third Session*, pp. 65–6 taken from *Le Monde* of 17 October 1964.
[2] See above, p. 112.

20 November, so that many of the fathers could go on to Bombay for the Eucharistic Congress. The Secretariat for Unity had, therefore, plenty of time in which to revise the declaration on Religious Liberty so that it could be brought back for further debate and finally promulgated. But, in fact, nothing more was heard of this important document until Tuesday, 17 November, when this session had only three more days to run. This was cutting it fine; but the fathers were told that a vote would be taken on the Thursday so that, if favourable, the declaration could be promulgated on the Saturday at the final public session. But this put the fathers into some difficulty, for the new Schema was very different from the previous one. It had now been separated from the Schema on Ecumenism and had become an independent declaration containing a good deal of new material. And there were only two days in which to read it and discuss it, both among themselves and in the Council. It was, therefore, not surprising that some of the bishops felt that they could not give due consideration to this important document in so short a time, and asked that it should be left over to the next session.

But why did it come so late? There seems to be no doubt that the Secretariat for Unity had completed their work by the middle of October, but that the powerful minority, who were dead against the Schema, had used their privileged positions to prevent the printers from handling it until it was really too late to get it through. On Wednesday, 18 November, a petition was read out demanding more time. This was said to have been signed by 200 bishops – less than 10 per cent of the whole number. Then on the following day Cardinal Tisserant announced, on behalf of the presidents, that it was too late to take a vote on this text and that it would, therefore, have to be deferred to the next session.

This statement was received with consternation. In 1963 the fathers had been told that there was no time to talk about

Religious Liberty but that they would have plenty of time to do
so in 1964. Then in September 1964 they were told, after some
days of discussion, that the text would be presented to them in
due course in a revised form. Nearly eight weeks later, and on
the last day but one of the Third Session, they were told that
the matter would now have to be deferred to 1965!

Since 'Xavier Rynne' is an assumed name, no one knows
whether the man who writes under this name was present in the
aula or not on the morning of this débacle; but his account is
vivid. Tisserant's words, he said

> 'were at first greeted by a feeble burst of applause from the
> minority bishops, but this was at once drowned by a wave of
> grumbling, protests and commotion which spread throughout the
> hall. One would have to go back to one of the early church
> Councils, that of Trent, for example, when an enraged bishop
> pulled another's beard, to find a precedent for the scene of con-
> sternation, outrage, and dismay that took place on this memor-
> able morning. The bishops felt cheated, betrayed, insulted and
> humiliated.'[1]

My own impression, having been present in S. Peter's that morning, is that this account is a bit exaggerated. But, all the same,
the decision not to allow a vote on this question made many of
the bishops very unhappy. Twice before they had been disappointed over this declaration; many of them had promised
their people that a statement on Religious Liberty would be
made this session. Now everything was to be postponed once
more.

Of all national groups, those who felt most strongly about it
were the Americans, and within a few moments a crowd of
bishops had collected round Cardinal Meyer who was busy
getting up a petition to the Pope to allow a vote to be taken.
Within an hour 800 signatures to this petition had been ob-

[1] *The Third Session*, p. 258. Later (on p. 259) he says that 'pandemonium
broke loose on the council floor'; but this is quite untrue.

tained, and before long there were 1,400, representing two-thirds of the Council. As I walked through the crowds milling about in the transepts, I met my friend John Wright, the Bishop of Pittsburgh, who nodded to me and said: 'You'd better go and have a word with your friend upstairs.' But the friend upstairs had made up his mind not to override the presidential decision and nothing further was done. The draft declaration on Religious Liberty was once more put in the cupboard for another nine months, and a lot of bishops returned to their homes bitterly disappointed.

A good deal of the Third Session was taken up with problems of the ministry – bishops, priests, religious, missionaries, and so on. It was a relief, therefore, to turn to certain problems which especially touched upon the life of the laity – their status in the Church, the education of their children and problems concerning holy matrimony.

In the ecumenical movement there has been a good deal of talk about the laity in recent years. The problems of ministry and all that it involves lie at the very heart of all talk about Christian Unity; but you cannot discuss ministry without discussing the whole problem of the nature of the Church, the People of God, and therefore of the laity as much as the clergy. The reformed Churches are well aware of the problems of the laity, and a good deal of work has been done to think out what part the laity must play in the whole mission of the Church.

In the reformed Churches reference is often made to the two expressions used by S. Peter in connection with the People of God (clerical and lay) whom he calls a 'royal priesthood' and a 'holy priesthood', thus emphasising the fact that the priesthood of Christ is continued not just in those who are set apart as priests, but in the whole Christian community. From this has developed the phrase 'the priesthood of all believers', which, so long as it is used in its true sense, and not to mean that there is no need for an ordained ministry, is a very important element in any kind of ecclesiology.

> 'The doctrine of the priesthood of the laity [writes Dr Alan Richardson] is in the fullest sense a biblical doctrine; but its content is far richer than that which is generally understood by the phrase "the priesthood of all believers". It was, indeed, necessary at the Reformation to stress that every individual Christian man or woman had through Christ direct access to God, apart entirely from the offices of any human intermediary: there is one Mediator only. This basic truth of the Gospel had been obscured by medieval sacerdotalism. The expression "the priesthood of all believers" represents a truth that must always be reasserted in face of the pretensions of all forms of priestcraft. But the expression is usually taken to mean simply that every man is his own priest; whereas the biblical conception of the priesthood of the laity is much more profound than this. It means that the Church is the appointed priest-nation to the "Gentile" world, i.e. to all that is not-Church; that the Church is responsible before God for "the world" and all its concerns, and that every individual Christian should strive to be a priest to the "Gentiles". The problem of evangelism in the secular world would lose much of its intractability if the "lay-folk" of the churches would take seriously the biblical teaching concerning their calling and office as laymen in the Church of God.'[1]

This sort of thing has become reasonably familiar to Anglicans and Protestants who are using lay people more and more in teaching, worship, mission and in the governance of the Church. It was, therefore, of great interest to us to see how the Roman Catholic Church would handle the problem of the laity.

As with the bishops and the religious, the laity have a whole chapter to themselves in the Constitution on the Church. This contains much that is biblically sound. It speaks of the People of God sharing in the priestly, prophetic and kingly functions of Christ (§ 31). It describes the lay apostolate as a participation in

[1] Alan Richardson, *An Introduction to the Theology of the New Testament* (London, 1958), p. 302.

the redemptive mission of the Church itself (§ 33). The priestly function of the laity lies in their offering their lives and their work as a spiritual sacrifice to God (§ 34), the prophetic function in their acting as witnesses to their faith (§ 35), and their kingly function by helping to spread the kingdom and laws of Christ in the world (§ 36). But, after saying all this, the chapter tries to put the laity in their proper place by saying that lay people must 'promptly accept, in Christian obedience, the decisions of their pastors since they are the representatives of Christ' (§ 37), though it allows dialogue between clergy and laity for the well-being of the Church.

It was on the basis of this chapter that the Schema on 'The Apostolate of the Laity' was drawn up. It dealt with the apostolic vocation of the laity, of the duties of lay people in different walks of life, of the aims to be sought, of various lay associations (with special reference to Catholic Action), of control of the laity by bishops and priests though with some reference to dialogue and to ecumenical co-operation.

This draft was not considered very satisfactory by the Council and was severely criticised by the observers. Many of the bishops thought it all very clerical and patronising. There was an old saying that the layman's job was 'to pray, pay and obey', and this Schema smacked a little of that mentality. 'There is no hope for any apostolate of the laity', said Archbishop D'Souza of Bhopal, 'if they are always to remain under the thumb of clerics.' 'Clericalism', said Archbishop Kozlowiecki of Lusaka, 'is the Enemy No. 1 in the Church', after saying which he started going about Rome in an open-necked shirt and grey flannel trousers under the very eye of Ottaviani and the Holy Office.

It was soon realised that this first text was disappointing and unworthy, and, after a few days debate it was sent back for revision. When it came up again in 1965 it had been improved enough to get through the Council; but, even so, many felt that not much progress had been made. 'Laity and clergy alike', wrote Dermot de Trafford, 'are faced with an enormous problem of adult education if they are to bring home to the people of God that they are the Church, and Christ depends upon them as his apostles.'[1]

In the Schema on the Laity so much had been said about the Christian home, and married life, and the nurture of children in the Christian faith, that it was perhaps inevitable that two other subjects should follow on, one on Christian Education and one on Christian Marriage. The first of these did not detain the Council fathers for very long; but the second was naturally regarded as of the greatest importance.

There is no point at which the tension between Romans and non-Romans is more painful than in the matter of mixed marriages. It would, as Cardinal Frings said on another occasion, be very much easier if people of different religious allegiance did not fall in love with one another. But, unfortunately, they do, and in so doing raise a number of very difficult problems.

There are, of course, many different kinds of mixed marriages according to the strength of the convictions of each of the two contracting parties. It quite often happens that, in the matter of religion, one party is very much more committed than the other. But – at any rate so far as England is concerned – the rules laid down by the Roman Catholic Church are the same for all. Before any member of the Roman Church can marry anyone outside his Communion, he (or she) must promise that all children which may result from the marriage shall be baptised and educated in the Roman Catholic faith. The non-Roman party is also made to promise, 'sincerely and openly', that she (or he) agrees with this and will put no obstacles in the way of the other party fulfilling his religious duties and obligations.

[1] *The Tablet*, 15 January 1966.

This, of course, raises very real difficulties and often much unhappiness. We know that the Roman Church has laid down strict rules on this matter. Believing herself to be the only true Church, she regards it as her duty to see that no soul is lost by becoming separated from that Church. She feels that she must, therefore, ensure that children of any Roman Catholic parent are brought up as Roman Catholics; and the only way to do this is to see that, before a marriage takes place, both parties agree that this should be so. This attitude looks simple enough, but in fact it often fails in its objective because it makes no allowance for the convictions and consciences of other people, and sometimes ends up in producing the very opposite of what was intended.

So far as mixed marriages in England are concerned it is, no doubt, true that, more often than not, the Roman Catholic partner is more committed (and certainly more disciplined) than the other. But this is not always so. If we take the example of a keen Roman Catholic boy wanting to marry a rather half-hearted Anglican girl, there is not much problem. The girl will probably not care very much where the children are baptised and brought up, and, if her husband insists that they should go to his church, that is all right to her. But supposing, as often happens, the parts are reversed and it is the young man who is really not much interested, and the girl who is anxious that the children should be christened at her parish church and be brought up as she was. Here the problem becomes exceedingly acute and may well end up with the children going nowhere, since the father won't send them to his church and the mother can't send them to hers. Against this it may be argued that the girl made the promises freely, that no one could force her to make them against her will. But it does not generally work out as simply as this. Great pressure may have been put on the girl by the boy's parents, and what girl wants to start off her married life by having a major row with her in-laws? So what is she to do? She can sign away her rights for the sake of peace and a church wedding, or she can stick up for her rights and have a marriage in a registry office – unless, of course, she can persuade the young man to be married in an Anglican church.

But the problem is even more difficult than this. If the girl stands out for her rights and insists on being married in an Anglican church (or in no church at all), then the marriage is regarded as invalid by the Roman Catholic Church. This means that, if the husband should prove to be unfaithful and desert his wife for someone else, he can be married to that person in a Roman Catholic Church with the full customary ceremonial since he is treated as a bachelor. The girl, on the other hand, could not be re-married in an Anglican Church since the Anglican Church would regard her former marriage, even if performed in a registry office, as a true and valid marriage.

Things of this kind may not happen very often, but the question is one of principle, not of numbers. What right has one Church to override the conscientious scruples of a member of another Church? What right has any Church to exercise authority (in requiring promises) over those who are not members of it? How does this system fit in with the words of the Declaration on Religious Liberty which say: 'Every family, as a society endowed with its own basic rights, has the right to organise its own domestic religious life under the direction of the parents. *Theirs is the right to determine the kind of religious instruction to be given to their children.*' Surely this must mean that, if the parents feel that it would be best for the children to attend an Anglican or Methodist Sunday School, they have the right to do so. Indeed, what else could it mean? But it also means that the Roman Catholic Church will now have to show whether it really believes in Religious Liberty or not.

In view of all this, the observers were most interested to see what the Council was prepared to do about mixed marriages. During the course of the year the fathers had received copies of a draft statement on Holy Matrimony. This was called a 'Votum', because what they were asked to approve was not a decree but certain principles upon which changes in Canon Law could be made.

On the question of mixed marriages the Votum declared: 'In order to give more appropriate consideration to the condition of the persons involved, as regards mixed marriages, saving the demands of divine law, canonical laws concerning the impediments of mixed religion and disparity of worship are to be adjusted in the light of the special norms laid down by the Sacred Council in reference to Ecumenism.' This was a bit vague, and many of us wondered what these 'special norms' were. However, in an appendix to the draft Votum some of the points which the fathers had sent in in writing were given. These showed that many of the bishops were fully aware of the difficulties, and realised that some relaxation of the present rules was necessary. Some pointed out that non-Roman Catholics had as much right as anyone else to claim conscientious scruples about the education of their children. Others questioned the legality of the Roman Catholic Church claiming the right to exact promises from members of other Churches. Many thought the present regulations far too rigid, and called for greater flexibility. Many asked that, before Canon Law was revised, some discussion with the 'separated brethren' should be held.

As a result of the points made by the fathers in writing, the Votum had been considerably revised. In its new form the passage on mixed marriages ran as follows:

'In accordance with the decrees on Religious Liberty and on Ecumenism . . . the following points are to be observed:
'In all mixed marriages . . . the catholic partner is to be seriously enjoined and must sincerely promise that he or she will see that

all children will be baptized and brought up as catholics, so far
as he is able (*in quantum poterit*).

'With regard to the promise, which is to be made by the catholic
partner alone, the non-catholic partner is to be informed about
this at a suitable time, and his or her consent obtained that he or
she is not opposed to it.

'The non-catholic partner must also be informed about the ends
and nature of marriage, and neither partner must have any
reservations about this matter.'

The passage went on to say that, in future, a mixed marriage,
so long as both parties are baptised, may be celebrated in the
course of the Mass, and that the excommunication required by
Canon Law against those who have contracted a marriage
before a non-Catholic minister shall be discontinued.

If all this were carried out, it would greatly ease the tension
between the Roman Catholic and other Churches. But some of
the bishops were – perhaps not unnaturally – worried about
the possible effects of such new legislation.

Among those who expressed such concern was Archbishop
Heenan, who addressed the Council on 20 November, speaking
on behalf of the whole hierarchy of England and Wales. At
first he declared the Votum to be 'good, indeed, excellent' and,
with true pastoral concern, he showed how important it was
that non-Catholics approaching the Church to discuss the
problems of matrimony should receive a warm and sympathetic
welcome. He, therefore, said that he hoped very much that
everything would be done, with music, candles, flowers and so
on, to make the wedding day 'both beautiful and happy even
though the marriage is a mixed marriage'. He then went on to
tell the fathers that his experiences as a parish priest in London
had convinced him that it was rare to find the non-Catholic
partner of a mixed marriage to be a really active member of any
religious community. 'For this reason', he went on, 'the promises to bring up the children as Catholics rarely caused difficulty.' This, of course, is partly true. There are a great many

lapsed Anglicans, just as there are a great many lapsed Roman Catholics, in England today. But the problem lies not with the lapsed, the indifferent and the careless, but with the minority who do care a great deal. For them the archbishop suggested that special rules might be drawn up; but he did not think the problem a very difficult one. 'We must not forget', he said, 'that it need be in no way against the conscience of a non-Catholic to agree to the children being brought up as Catholics. Other Christian Churches do not claim to be the one true Church.'[1] On the other hand, quite a number of 'non-Catholics' might find it very much against their conscience to allow their children to be brought up to make that kind of claim.

In spite of the importance of the subject, especially for its ecumenical implications, very little time was allowed for the discussion of this Votum, and only fourteen bishops spoke about it. Some of them, including Archbishop Conway of Armagh, were greatly alarmed by it, and declared that it would be madness even to agree to these proposals as suitable to be passed on to the appropriate authority. But most of the fathers thought otherwise, and the Council agreed, by 1,592 to 426, to send the text, together with the observations made upon it, to the Holy Father for him to decide what action should be taken.

The Vatican remained silent for sixteen months; but during the Fourth Session there were indications that the rights of non-Romans in regard to the education of their children, in spite of what had been said in the 'Declaration on Religious Liberty', were going to be ignored. In the earlier drafts of the Schema on 'The Church in the Modern World' there had been a sentence which declared that 'the parents' right of procreation, and their right to educate their children according to the dictates of their conscience, especially as regards religion, must be fully safeguarded'. The fact that this sentence was omitted from the

---

[1] The full text of this speech will be found in *English Bishops at the Council: The Third Session*, pp. 130–4.

final text was an indication that anything which might encourage non-Romans to think that their rights were going to
receive consideration was now being withdrawn.

The official statement was made on 18 March, 1966, not, as
had been intended, in the form of a papal pronouncement, or
motu proprio, but in the form of instructions from the Holy
Office. This statement confirmed the fears which many of us
had. It still demanded that the 'non-Catholic' partner shall
promise not to place any obstacles in the way of children being
baptised and educated as Roman Catholics, and declared that
such promises should normally be given in writing. It does, however, allow the 'ordinary' to give permission for such promises
to be made verbally, though what difference this can make to
anyone with any conscientious convictions about the solemnity
of any promise is hard to see. It also says that the bishop, if he
knows that the conscience of the non-Roman partner is
troubling him, may 'refer the case with all relevant details to
the Holy See'. But this leaves power in the hands of the Roman
Church and still runs counter to what the Council has declared
about the basic rights and liberties of the individual.

The statement must, therefore, be regarded as disappointing
to those who had hoped that the wishes of the Council would be
observed. There are, however, one or two points which show
that doors may still be slightly open. For one thing the text,
which refers to 'our predecessor of happy memory John XXIII',
was obviously drawn up in the form of a *motu proprio* with all the
authority which that would carry with it. The fact that the
Pope decided not to sign it and handed it over to Ottaviani is
an indication that it may be treated as an 'interim' measure.
Secondly, it must be remembered that 'mixed marriages' include not only those with members of more orthodox Christian
Churches, but also with Mormons, Pentacostalists and members
of strange sects whose ideas of the nature of Christian marriage
may be very different from ours. Thirdly, it was stated in the

Council, by Cardinal Heenan and others, that whereas the rules should normally be strict, special regulations might be drawn up to try to make things a little easier where one of the partners to the marriage is a practising member of another Christian Church. We all very much hope that something along these lines may be done; otherwise a serious blow will have been struck to confidence in the Roman Catholic Church's wish to be on better terms with her neighbours or to take seriously her own statements about Religious Liberty.

Two other subjects occupied the Council for some time during the Third Session. One was Divine Revelation, and the other The Church in the Modern World.

It will be remembered that, in 1962, the Theological Commission had offered the Council a draft called 'The double source of revelation'. This had been roughly handled and was eventually discarded, Pope John promising to set up a new mixed commission to prepare a wholly new text.[1] It was this new text, with the title 'On Divine Revelation', which was presented to the fathers by Archbishop Florit of Florence on 30 September. This was at once seen to be a great improvement on what had been offered in 1962. Getting away from the language of Trent and Vatican I, it links together the Bible, Tradition and the Teaching Authority, or Magisterium, of the Church as the means whereby the truth about God is communicated to man. It adopts a much more modern and reasonable attitude towards the Bible, admitting that it was written in the language of the age and used the 'literary forms' which were then customary – a hint at the science of 'Formgeschichte'. It laid great emphasis on the study of the Bible, and on the importance of looking at the Scriptures as a whole and not just as a collection of isolated texts. It introduced what Oscar Cullmann called 'this marvellous phrase' which says that 'in the Holy Scriptures, the Father who is in heaven constantly

[1] See above, p. 55.

meets his children and speaks with them'.[1] It stated that the interpretation of the Bible must be dynamic and not static, encouraged the preparation (where possible with the help of non-Roman Catholics) of translations into all languages, and laid upon clergy, religious and the faithful laity the duty of regular and diligent Bible-reading.

All this was, naturally, well received in the observers' box. Brought up, as many of them had been, on the idea that the Bible is the final authority in all matters of faith and morals, it was good to see so much reverence shown to the Scriptures in this Schema. Of course many of them would have liked it to go further. Professor Cullmann, while praising the text as a vast improvement on what had gone before, regretted that, according to Roman Catholic doctrine, the Church could never be judged by the Bible, and wished that what he called this 'over-againstness of Scripture' had been given more weight. But he, like everyone else, appreciated the way in which Bible, Tradition and Magisterium had been linked together.

In the Council, however, there was, of course, a group which was bitterly opposed to the new approach to what they regarded as the infallible and incontrovertible right of the Church to say what shall be believed and done. So strongly did these men feel about it that they put up Archbishop Franic of Split to introduce a minority report disagreeing with the text as presented.

The debate really turned on two points. One concerned the magisterium of the Church. Some wished to say that it was the Church's job to tell people the truth, and that once the Church had spoken there was no appeal. Both Bible and Tradition were at the disposal of the Church in formulating truth, and she was free to draw upon either according to her requirements. Others wished the whole question of divine revelation to be studied in its integrity with due emphasis being given to the various ways

[1] O. Cullmann, 'The Bible in the Council' in *Dialogue on the Way*, p. 136.

in which God's truth had been made known to men. The other subject concerned the way in which the Bible was to be studied and interpreted. Some were for maintaining an old-fashioned 'fundamentalist' approach, which would have lost them the respect of the world of scholarship; others were for allowing scholars to search for the truth, using all means at their command. These latter found their mouthpiece in Abbot Butler who, at the end of his speech on 6 October, said:

'In the course of this almost miraculous Council we have done much to drive out that spirit of fear and excessive anxiety by which at times our labours were hindered. Today I say: Let us not be afraid of scholarly and historical truth. Let us not be afraid that one truth may tell against another truth. Let us not be afraid that our scholars may be lacking in loyalty to the Church and to traditional doctrine. One of two things is true: *either* there is a world-wide conspiracy of scholars to undermine the bases of Christian faith (and a man who can believe that can believe anything); *or* the aim of our scholars is to reach the full, objective and real truth of the Gospel tradition. In this task they play a dual role: they are loyal Catholics; and they are at the same time scientific scholars whose first presupposition is honesty of investigation. Doubtless some will turn liberty into licence – but we must risk this for the sake of the greater good. Doubtless mistakes are made and will be made in this field – but it is one where trial and error are the road to truth. What we want is not the childish comfort which comes from averting our gaze from the truth, but a truly critical scholarship which will enable us to enter into "dialogue" with non-Catholic scholars.'[1]

Here was the voice of the true scholar, a man nurtured in the best Anglican tradition, trained in Classics and Theology at Oxford, one who thought as good theologians of every denomination think and who knew what harm would accrue to the Church of his adoption if the reactionary and unlearned minority were to be allowed to drag that Church down to the level of their little minds. It was because of the warmth and

[1] *English Bishops at the Council: Third Session*, p. 105.

depth of speakers like Abbot Butler that the Council finally adopted this new decree by 2,081 to 27.

The other great subject which the Council had to face in 1964 was 'The Church in the Modern World'. This long, complicated, controversial and comprehensive document owes its origin partly to a speech made by Cardinal Suenens on 4 December, 1962. The Council was then discussing, rather perfunctorily and wearily, a draft constitution on the Church which was proving quite inadequate and unworthy of the subject. It was then that the Cardinal Archbishop of Brussels-Malines made his great speech. He said that, as Vatican I had been the Council of the Primacy, so Vatican II would have to be the Council of the Church. When the Council finally stated its views on the Church there would need to be a dual approach – *ad intra*, that is, on its own internal affairs; and *ad extra*, on its mission to and relation with the world. The whole world, he said, was looking to the Church for help in its many problems, and it would be disastrous if the Church were to fail to give this help to a suffering, frightened and perplexed world. This meant that, in addition to a constitution on Ecclesiology, the Council would have to consider drawing up a totally new document to deal with such things as Church and State, the population-explosion, world poverty and hunger, peace and war, and a hundred other things.

There was no doubt that the Council warmly approved of this suggestion, and, throughout 1963 and 1964, a commission worked hard on this under the presidency of Bishop Guano of Leghorn and with Fr Bernard Häring as its secretary. As a result of their labours a draft on 'The Church in the Modern World' was now laid before the fathers for discussion. It contained a preface followed by four chapters:

1. On the whole vocation of man.
2. On the Church dedicated to the service of God and man.

3. On the conduct of Christians in the world in which they live.

4. On the chief duties to be fulfilled by Christians of our day. These four rather vague headings concealed a mass of very controversial and highly inflammable material, including Religious Freedom, World Poverty, the Equality of Women, Family Planning, Industrial Relations, Nuclear Warfare, Atheistic Communism, Racism, Conscientious Objection, and many others.

The Schema, with its accompanying document of *Adnexa* or additional material, was, on the whole, well received. Many of the fathers felt the necessity of giving some help to the world, and, although they might not approve of all that was here stated, at least they were prepared to discuss it. Others felt more doubtful. The Schema raised so many controversial matters that there did not seem much hope of the fathers reaching agreement on anything of importance. Others were afraid that many of the subjects were beyond their competence. Trained as they were to talk about theology, they did not feel very happy when they were asked to express their opinions on medical, scientific, psychological and political matters. As one of the English bishops whom I encountered in the side-aisles of S. Peter's said to me: 'You can just imagine the sort of hot air we shall get blown at us in there.'

One thing, however, the draft constitution did was to answer the question which everyone was asking: 'Is there going to be a Fourth Session?' In view of the mountain of material which this celebrated Schema 13 had laid before them, there was now no doubt whatever that the fathers would be required to return to Rome in 1965.

CHAPTER SIX

1965: *The Last Lap*

DURING THE EARLY PART OF 1965 THE EFFECTS OF
the Council were beginning to show themselves. The decree on
Ecumenism had been officially promulgated on 21 November,
1964, and early in December the English hierarchy issued a
statement giving instructions as to how Roman Catholics could
join in worship with members of other Christian Churches.
These were only tentative proposals, as the *Directorium*, which is
to give practical effect to the decree, was not yet published; but
one of the things which they did was to encourage not only
joint meetings but joint acts of worship during the Week of
Prayer for Christian Unity which is held each year. This meant
that, in the following January, some very remarkable scenes
were witnessed. The one in which I took part was held in Leeds
Town Hall on 21 January. As soon as I received a copy of the
statement issued by the English hierarchy, I made arrangements for the Town Hall to be booked, and invited the Bishop of
Leeds to join us. As a result partly of good advertising, and partly
of a desire to make this a really big occasion, we had the Town
Hall packed, an overflow meeting in a neighbouring Methodist
church, and many turned away. The ceremony began with
some speeches, but it ended with an act of worship – not unlike
an Anglican Evensong with lessons, the Magnificat, hymns and

prayers. People were much impressed by the vast numbers who attended, and by the fact that, for the first time, obvious Roman Catholics were there in force. This gave a real sense of progress, of a new friendship, of the breaking-down of ancient barriers of fear and distrust, of Christian solidarity in the face of so much indifference and neglect of the things of God.

Within the Roman Church itself people were having to face big changes in the form of public worship with the introduction of the vernacular. Early in February I spent a night with the Franciscans at East Bergholt, where I gave a talk to the friars on the Council. The following morning when I attended Mass in their chapel and heard the familiar words: 'I will go unto the altar of God: even unto the God of my joy and gladness,' I began to wonder where I was. Many of us, however, felt that the translation used in the new services was not always very good. A leading article in *The Tablet* pleaded for the use of the language of the Book of Common Prayer on the grounds that it was of fine quality, had been in continuous use for 400 years, and would form a link between Rome and other parts of the Christian Church. But as Cardinal Godfrey had opposed the restoration of the Chalice to the laity on the grounds that it would appear to be giving way to the Anglicans,[1] so a wholesale borrowing of language from the Book of Common Prayer might appear to some as in the nature of unconditional surrender. Consequently, in some of the English liturgies you get phrases like: 'Lamb of God, who take away the sins of the world,' which sounds very rough to ears accustomed to the voice of Cranmer.

In February the World Council of Churches issued a statement about their relations with Rome. This was drawn up at their meeting at Enugu in West Africa where, no doubt, the discussions at Rummelsberg were reported. This statement assumed that dialogue between the World Council and the Roman Church would now take place, and a Joint Commission

[1] See above, p. 44.

was set up to discuss such things as ways of collaborating in philanthropic, social and international affairs, theological study on Faith and Order, discussion of problems which inevitably cause tension – such as mixed marriages, proselytism and religious liberty – and common concerns about the life and mission of the Church. This Commission has already started its work, but, of course, no reports have yet been published.

Meanwhile preparations were going on for the Fourth Session of the Council which was due to meet on Holy Cross Day, 14 September. There was certainly a heavy programme to be considered; but the commissions had been working like beavers to get the material into a form in which it would be acceptable to the fathers, and there was real hope that the end was now in sight. The seventy-three drafts which the preparatory commission had considered had now been reduced to sixteen, of which five had been promulgated – Liturgy and Means of Communication in 1963, and The Church, Ecumenism and the Eastern Churches in 1964. This left the following:

1. Religious Liberty.
2. The Church in the Modern World.
3. The Missionary Activity of the Church.
4. Priestly Life and Ministry.
5. Divine Revelation.
6. The Apostolate of the Laity.
7. Pastoral Duties of Bishops.
8. Adaptation and Renewal of the Religious Life.
9. Formation of Priests.
10. Christian Education.
11. The Relation of the Church to Non-Christian Religions.

All of these had been presented in 1964, and some of them would, no doubt, be dealt with fairly quickly. But the first two were likely to arouse a good deal of opposition, and no one quite knew how any of the others was likely to fare.

It was, therefore, impossible to say whether this Fourth Session would be the last one or not, and when we met in Rome in September the air was thick with rumours. Some said that the commissions had done their work so well that the whole thing could be polished off in a few weeks; others said that the Council would go on until Christmas and meet again in the new year; yet others believed that there would have to be a Fifth Session in the autumn of 1966. Most of the fathers were by now hoping that this would be the last session and that it would be over by Christmas. But, to do so, things would have to move pretty quickly. There would probably be fewer general assemblies in order to leave more time for the commissions to try to get the material into an acceptable form. There would certainly have to be fewer speeches and less repetition. In fact, Felici, the general secretary, sent out instructions in July telling the fathers that, if they wanted to speak on either Religious Liberty or The Church in the Modern World, they must send the text of their speech (or a summary of it) to him before 9 September (i.e. five days before the Council opened). This, though perhaps a necessary, was not at all a popular, move. Many of the fathers complained that discussion or debate becomes impossible if all the speeches have to be written well in advance, and many thought the whole thing a ruse to enable the secretaries to suppress anything which they didn't approve of.

There was, therefore, a good deal of uncertainty and speculation in the air when we met. But this was partly settled when the Pope spoke to us at the opening session. Four times in the course of his speech he referred to 'this final session', though he gave no indication as to when it would end, whether before or after Christmas. In fact, the Council was brought to a successful conclusion on 8 December, as many had prophesied.

In addressing the fathers, the Pope began by giving thanks to God for having brought them to 'the present final session' of the Council. 'We come to it', he said, 'with a strong and common determination of loyalty to the Word of God, and in a deep

brotherly adherence to the catholic faith. We meet for a full and
fervent study of the manifold problems regarding our religion,
and particularly the nature and the mission of the Church of
God. We unanimously desire to forge still stronger bonds of
union with those Christian brethren who are still separated
from us, and we mean to address to the world a heartfelt
message of friendship and of salvation.' This showed that Pope
Paul still had very much in mind the two-fold objective of the
Council – Renewal and Reunion. Several times in this speech
he referred to the 'separated brethren', and each time he turned
slightly towards us and made a small gesture in his shy,
nervous way, by lifting his left hand a little.

The speech lasted forty-three minutes and covered a good
deal of familiar ground. The surprising announcement came
towards the end, when the Pope informed us that he was about
to set up an Episcopal Synod. Something along these lines had
been suggested in the debate on Collegiality in 1963, but
further progress had been made when the Council was discussing the Schema on 'Bishops and their Dioceses', the first
chapter of which dealt with relations between the bishops and
the sacred congregations of the Roman Curia. One of the things
which the bishops wanted to do all along was to get power away
from the Curia, and so make it possible for them to have greater
freedom and independence in the planning of their work. This
desire came up in the debates on the Church, on Seminaries and
on Missions. As early as 16 October, 1963, Bishop Holland, then
coadjutor of Portsmouth, had suggested, on behalf of the English hierarchy, that something in the nature of an Episcopal
Synod should be set up as 'a sort of continuation of the spirit
which inspires this Council'. A few weeks later Maximos IV
had declared, in his forceful way, that it was no longer possible
or advisable for the Pope to try to run the Church with a handful of men in Rome – mostly cardinals who were a relic of the
old days when the Pope took the advice of the parish clergy of

Rome. Things were now totally different, and the Pope needed
to have the information and advice of men from all over the
world. In this Maximos was supported by such men as Cardinals Frings and Lercaro, though opposition naturally came
from some of the Roman cardinals in whose hands power now
lies.[1]

The idea of a senate or synod of bishops found a place in the
Schema on the 'Pastoral Office of Bishops' where a 'deliberative
body' is envisaged together with a complete reorganisation of
the various offices, known as 'dicasteries'. This suggestion was
still *sub iudice*, as this decree had not yet been voted upon; but
the Pope decided to force the issue, and, in his opening address,
announced 'the setting up, in accordance with the wishes of the
Council, of an Episcopal Synod, composed of bishops to be
chosen for the most part by the Episcopal Conferences [i.e the
local hierarchies] and approved by us, which will be convened
according to the needs of the Church, by the Roman Pontiff,
for consultation and collaboration when this is needed'. The
Pope was obviously pleased to do this. He commended the plan
to the intercessions of the Virgin Mary, and said that he
thought it full of splendid opportunities.

Having made this promise, which was loudly applauded, Paul
wasted no time. The next morning (15 September) he came to
the *aula* and caused to be read out, by Cardinal Marella, the
motu proprio outlining the constitution of the Synod. It was to be
composed of the patriarchs, metropolitans and major archbishops, a number of bishops elected by their fellows, some
religious elected by the Conference of Superiors, and the Cardinal Presidents of the congregations. The Pope reserved the
right to nominate a further 15 per cent, and the whole Synod
was expected to consist of about 150–160 members. Three
points about it are important: (1) that it will be a *permanent* body,
a kind of continuation of the Council; (2) that it will be a *legisla-*

[1] X. Rynne, *The Second Session*, pp. 95, 180–6.

F

tive body with power to enact decrees which will be binding on
the Church; and (3) that it will be *representative* in that the
majority of the members will be there by election and not *ex
officio*.

This was seen by the observers as a very important move.
Perhaps the thing which struck us most was that, for the first
time, a democratic element had found its way into the government of the Church of Rome. It was also thought to sound the
death-knell to the series of 'ecumenical' councils. The future of
councils had often been discussed during the last few years, for
the thing was obviously becoming unwieldly and almost un-
manageable. At the Council of Trent in the sixteenth century
attendance had varied between 34 and 255. At the First
Vatican Council less than 800 had attended. But now there
were 2,300 members, and new sees being created all the time.
Should another Council be held in, say, fifty years time, there
might well be over 3,000 people qualified to attend, so making
any rational discussion virtually impossible. Theologians told
us that the idea of Church Councils, being of divine institution,
could never be abolished; but they thought that a synod could
do a great deal to remove the necessity for further meetings of
the Council.

But though the observers (and the non-Roman Christian
world generally) could applaud the document which announced
the formation of the Synod, they felt less pleased about the
other papal pronouncement which appeared about the same
time, an encyclical letter called 'Mysterium Fidei' published
just before the Council reassembled. This dealt with the
Eucharist, and was obviously intended as a rebuke to certain
statements which had been issued by theologians. Some of these
had expressed doubt about the wisdom of allowing private
Masses, while others had come near to denying the Church's
official doctrine of Transubstantiation, substituting such words
as 'transignification' or 'transfiguration' to describe what takes

place in the Eucharist. The letter refers to 'false opinions' which had been expressed, and the belief was that the Pope had especially in mind a group of Dutch theologians whose writings had caused some ferment. Against all this Paul comes down heavily, setting out again all the traditional doctrines about the sacrifice of the Mass, post-Eucharistic devotions, and Transubstantiation, defining the last of these in the words: 'after the change of the substance or nature of the bread and wine into the Body and Blood of Christ, nothing remains of the bread and wine but the appearances'.

All this was disappointing to those who felt that the Council was really trying to break away from mediaeval scholasticism and Tridentine theology and speak to the modern world in language which it could understand. Although the practical suggestions contained in the Constitution on the Liturgy were being put into operation, it looked as if the theological and doctrinal foundations of the Constitution were being ignored. 'Pope Paul's encyclical on the celebration of the Eucharist', wrote Fr Gregory Baum, 'is regarded by many as a sign that the Pope, by stressing the Council of Trent over against the teaching of Vatican II, wishes to slow down the movement of renewal and reform. . . . Since Pope Paul's terminology is so different from the Constitution on the Liturgy, it is not easy to fit his encyclical harmoniously into the conciliar teaching of Vatican II.'[1]

The opening of the Fourth Session, therefore, produced mixed feelings. There was a feeling of assurance that the end was in sight; a feeling of satisfaction that the Pope had so quickly announced the setting up of the Synod; but a feeling of disappointment over the publication of 'Mysterium Fidei'. And behind all this was a nagging feeling about Pope Paul himself. Where does he stand? What is he really trying to do? How far is he in favour of reform, or how far is he falling into the clutches

[1] Article in *The Canadian Register* quoted in *Herder Correspondence*, 1965, p. 359.

of the 'old guard' who are using all their skill and determination
to stifle those movements which they can only see as a threat to
their own power? An interesting article in the American maga-
zine, *Time*, drew a contrast between Pope John and Pope Paul.
'John', it said, 'was an intuitive, charismatic prophet, who threw
open the doors and windows of the Church to let in fresh air,
without worrying about – or even fully understanding – the
consequences. By contrast, Paul is a detached and painstakingly
analytical technician who has left the windows open – but who
keeps checking the thermometer lest any cold drafts seep in.'[1]
Many people still had great hopes that Paul would, eventually,
justify himself and his apparently contradictory policies. But
there was growing anxiety. It was often said that thirty-two
years in Rome in the Vatican Secretariat of State had left their
mark on him, and had ineradicably developed in him the diplomatic instinct for caution, for the desire to see every side of
every question, and to listen to what everyone had to say, and
the fear of giving offence, especially to those near at hand.
There was much talk of this kind during the Fourth Session of
the Council, and those who had most faith in Pope Paul were at
pains to point out the difficulties which he had inherited in
having to steer to a successful conclusion a vast upheaval in the
Church which was not of his choosing. Here, perhaps, his
strength would lie.

After the opening ceremonies, the Council was allowed to
start straight away on the highly controversial subject of
Religious Liberty. Twice the fathers had come near to voting on
this, and twice it had been snatched from them. A third attempt
to do this would have meant a major disaster; so, on 15
September, Bishop de Smedt of Bruges presented the declaration in its new form. He pointed out that the fathers must bear
in mind the basis of the whole text, which was the dignity and

[1] *Time*, 24 September 1965, p. 56.

rights of man as a creature of God, and told them that there was really only one question which they would have to answer: 'Does each human individual or group enjoy the right to immunity from coercion in religious matters?'

The Schema which the fathers would now have to debate was divided into fifteen paragraphs. Many thought it far too long and discursive. There is, indeed, much repetition, and many rather vague statements; but perhaps those who had framed it felt that it would carry more respect if it appeared in the form of a 17-page pamphlet rather than as a broadsheet or a handful of propositions.

The declaration begins by referring to the general demand in the world for responsible freedom, a demand which must include religious freedom as well as other kinds. It goes on to declare that the human person as such has a right to religious freedom and that 'no one is to be forced to act in a manner contrary to his own beliefs, nor is anyone to be restrained from acting in accordance with his own beliefs, whether privately or publicly, whether alone or in association with others, within due limits'. Religious Liberty is not just a personal or individual thing; it is something which applies also to groups, whether these are minorities in a country which is predominantly of another part of the Christian Church, or whether they are Christians living in an atheistic or anti-Christian state. These groups must have the right to train and appoint ministers to serve them, to keep in touch with fellow-Christians in other countries, to build places of worship, to raise money for their maintenance, and publicly to teach the faith which they believe. Religious Liberty must apply also to the family, where 'parents have the right to determine, in accordance with their own religious beliefs, the kind of religious education that their children are to receive'.[1] The declaration then goes on to con-

[1] For the implications of this in the matter of mixed marriages, see above, pp. 140-2.

sider the duty of any government to protect the rights of
Christian minorities so long as they cause no trouble. Finally the
document deals with the biblical sanctions for the principle of
Religious Liberty.

Such was the document presented to the fathers on 15
September. That it was still a highly controversial matter is
shown by the fact that no less than sixty-four of the fathers contributed to the debate. Nearly half of these were cardinals, thirty
of whom spoke. Of these thirty, eighteen were in favour, seven
were against and five were doubtful.

All the old arguments against the declaration were trotted
out:

that only the Catholic Church has the right to preach the Gospel
(Cardinal Arriba y Castro);

that the 'Catholic' religion is the only one which is obviously true
(Cardinal Cooray);

that the *natural* right of the (Roman Catholic) Church is not to be
confused with the *positive* right of other religious groups (Cardinal
Florit);

that the Catholic Church has a true, natural and objective right
to liberty because of her divine origin and because of her divine
mission (Cardinal Ottaviani);

that the spreading of another 'religion' in a Catholic state is a
violation of public morality and injures the right which Catholics
enjoy not to have their faith endangered (Cardinal Browne);

that the text should be revised so as to grant to the one, true
Church religious liberty in the absolute sense, reserving to other
faiths religious tolerance according to circumstances of time and
place (Archbishop Tagle of Valparaiso speaking for a group of
forty-five bishops);

that if all men are given the right to a public profession of any
religion, this will be an insult to the Catholic Church (Bishop
Ferrevia of Lourenço Marques);

that the principles set forth in the Schema are completely unacceptable because they originated outside the Church and are in
open conflict with the consistent tradition of the Church (Archbishop Lefebvre of the Holy Ghost Fathers).

So much for the opposition. From the other side there were many strongly in favour of this declaration, and able to find good reasons for supporting it. They pointed out:

that it was a real answer to the requirements of modern times . . . the principles here formulated can give great impetus to ecumenism . . . any modifications in the text could give rise to serious doubts regarding the sincerity of the Church and the Council (Cardinal Spellman);

that the Schema answers the expectations of the Church and of the world . . . and need cause no fear (Cardinal Cushing);

that the presentation of this Schema should be an occasion of great joy, and that the work done by the Secretariat for Christian Unity in revising this text now leaves nothing more to be desired except the approval and promulgation of the document (Cardinal Ritter);

that the text is acceptable because it bases the right to religious liberty on the dignity of the human person (Cardinal Conway);

that the text is deserving of praise and should win moral unanimity in the vote of the Council (Bishop Sauvage of Annecy);

that although there are dangers in the régime of liberty, they must be overcome with positive means, since the dangers of a régime without liberty are still greater . . . that Religious Liberty will help to build a better world, and will arouse great hopes among the younger generation . . . and that this document is a necessary step on the road to sincere and effective ecumenism (Cardinal Cardijn, founder of the Jocist movement);

that the text is particularly deserving of praise in that it claims no special rights for the Catholic Church (Bishop Gran of Oslo).

Between these two points of view the debate oscillated until 22 September when de Smedt summed up what had been said and Felici put to the Council the question as to whether the present text of the declaration was acceptable as a basis for the document which would finally be presented when the points made in this discussion had been considered. This was passed by 1,997 votes to 224, and so another milestone on the road to Religious Liberty was reached.

The Secretariat for Unity now had about a month in which

to consider what had been said in debate and the various suggestions which had been sent in in writing. Then on 25 October
the final form of the declaration was placed before the fathers.
It was immediately clear that the members of the Secretariat
had been most scrupulous in trying to meet the objections of
those who wanted it to be made clear that, although granting
liberty to others, the Council believed that the Roman Church
was the true Church. Thus in the first paragraph a statement
was made that 'God has made known to mankind the way in
which men are to serve him, and thus be saved in Christ and
come to blessedness. We believe that this one true religion subsists in the Catholic and Apostolic Church, to which the Lord
Jesus committed the duty of spreading it abroad among men'.
(With which, of course, we should agree, though reserving the
right to believe that the Anglican Church is just as much a part
of the 'Catholic and Apostolic Church' as is the Church of
Rome.) Again, in the second paragraph, an addition was made
declaring the moral obligation on every man to seek the truth
and adhere to it when found. Thus, in a number of small ways,
the revised text was made a little more acceptable to those
fathers who feared that the whole thing would do great damage
to their Church. Even so there were many who felt unhappy
about it and could vote only *placet iuxta modum* when the time
came. So once more the Secretariat had to get to work on the
modi, and it was not until 19 November that they could present
the final text. This was passed by 1,954 to 249, and the declaration was proclaimed on 7 December.

This was a great triumph for people like Fr John Courtney
Murray, S.J., Bishop de Smedt and all those who had worked so
hard and so long to get the Council to make this declaration. It
had been a tough fight, for there were a good many of the
Council fathers who really believed that this document would
encourage the heresy of 'indifferentism', the belief that it didn't
much matter which Church you belonged to. It is fundamental

to the faith of a Roman Catholic that the Church to which he belongs is the only true Church, and that it is the will of God that everyone should be a member of it. It was, therefore, important that any declaration on Religious Liberty should not confuse people or lead them into false beliefs. The Church's faith in itself had to be safeguarded. But it was equally important that the Church should realise that not all can believe or accept what this Church teaches, and that they must have the right to practise that form of religion that seems to them to be the purest and the best. Religious Liberty is not like Toleration – something which the Church is generous enough to give to those who cannot agree with it; it is the natural and inalienable right of every man. This is something fundamental; and it is this that the Council has now declared.

A draft document on 'The Church in the Modern World' had been introduced in 1964 and a short debate on it had been held.[1] Many had greeted this Schema with delight, feeling how important it was for the Church to have some message to give to the world. It was sometimes said that a Schema of this kind was the only part of the Council's work in which Pope John was really interested. The world, he and many like him felt, was looking to the Church for guidance. Beset by so many problems, people turned wistfully, and perhaps not very hopefully, to the Church, asking for help. Would the Church be able to give it? Had the Church any real message to give to mankind? If so, what should she say?

This Schema was an attempt to answer these questions, and it was suggested that this was a matter on which Christians might well work together since, on so many matters which concerned the welfare of mankind, all Churches would want to say much the same kind of things. So the Schema says: 'We hope that, since our task is one and the same, we may also be heard

[1] See above, pp. 148-9.

by the beloved brethren of the communities of the Church that are separated from us, who confess the same Lord and Saviour of the world as we do, and who have themselves given not a few indications of equal concern.' Perhaps, as I have already indicated, it would have been better if those who compiled this Schema had asked not so much for the attention of the 'separated brethren' as for their collaboration; but perhaps this was too much to hope for. Anyhow, Christians of all denominations read this Schema, and listened to this debate, with the closest attention, realising that what Rome said on some of the issues involved would reverberate throughout the whole Christian world.

The amount of material in what came to be known as 'Schema 13' (though in fact no numbers were officially attached to any of the Schemata) was so great, and some of the issues were so controversial, that the Council did not manage to get much done during the Third Session. No Schema lent itself more to irrelevance, and the fathers kept being dragged down some sideline. One made it an occasion to deliver an attack on the theologians or *periti*, another pleaded that bishops should dress more simply, another attacked the *Index* of prohibited books, another advertised tourism, another preached patriotism. But, as the fathers ploughed their way through the discussion, two subjects kept coming up – one the question of Family Planning or Birth Control, the other the problem of warfare with nuclear weapons. These two subjects – commonly known as 'The Pill' and 'The Bomb' – tended to swamp everything else since they were both matters on which diametrically opposed views were held in the Council.

On the question of Flamily Planning the text read as follows:

'In regard to the number of their offspring, the final decision rests with the parents. But care must be taken that solutions are not broadcast nor imposed by civil authorities with little or no regard for morality, and which strive by any means whatever to put an end to the increasing population of the world or of a given country. But whenever circumstances so require, people should be informed about scientific advances the validity of which has been well established and their morality placed beyond doubt.'

This was fair enough; but, if the parents were to decide the number of their offspring, some method of keeping to the pre-determined number would be necessary. How is this to be done? What methods can be regarded as 'morally beyond doubt', and what are not? This was the real problem which, so far, the text had not really faced.

Some of the bishops probably had little idea how great the problem was. But others knew. Rather unexpectedly, it was the eighty-six-year-old patriarch, Maximos IV, who showed most knowledge of the subject. After referring to 'a break between the official doctrine of the Church and the contrary practice of the vast majority of Christian couples', he showed how this was causing much anxiety and often a sense of guilt which he called a 'crisis of conscience'. It was these people whom the Church must consider and try to help. Cardinals Léger, Suenens and Alfrink all supported him in pleading for a new approach to the problem. But Ottaviani put the opposite case. Saying that he was proud to be the eleventh of the twelve children of a labourer in a Roman bake-house, he hinted that if his parents had prac-tised any form of Family Planning he might not have been here to address the Council today. That was something which most of the Council would have regretted – for various reasons – but it was not a very strong argument for retaining the present policy.

On the problem of Peace and War the Schema points out that 'there is no true peace if wars are only postponed by a parity of weapons for spreading terror, rather than by a sin-cere spirit of co-operation and concord'. It then goes on to plead that disputes between nations must in future be settled by agreement rather than by arms, though it recognises a country's right to defend itself against aggression. On the sub-

ject of nuclear warfare it states that 'the use of arms, especially
nuclear weapons, whose effects are greater than can be
imagined, and therefore cannot reasonably be regulated by men,
exceeds all just proportion and must, therefore, be judged before
God and man as most wicked'. This was acclaimed by many of
the fathers; but it naturally caused some concern to the
American bishops who, with memories of Hiroshima and Naga-
saki, were a little doubtful whether they wanted their country's
actions to be described as 'before God and man *most wicked*'.
No country represented at the Council had anything like so
many weapons of large-scale destruction as the United States.
Were the American bishops to go home and tell their Government to get rid of them?

Thus, on these two controversial matters, the fathers were
obviously going to be very much divided, and a lot of revision
would have to take place before an acceptable text would be
produced. But, after beating about the bush for a bit, the Third
Session came to an end, and the Pope and many of the bishops
rushed off to Bombay where they would see enough over-
crowding and poverty to make them think again about the
problem of Birth Control.

In 1965 the fathers had to turn their attention again to
Schema 13 and all its problems. During the interval it had been
so much revised that it was practically a new document which
we now had to study. It was also very much longer, having been
enlarged from 25 paragraphs to 106. After an Introduction and
a Preparatory Statement, the document was divided into two
parts, one on 'The Church and the Condition of Man', and the
other on 'Some Practical Problems', dealing with Marriage,
Culture, Economics, Politics and War. This Schema was placed
before the Council on 21 September, 1965, by Archbishop
Garrone of Toulouse, who spoke on behalf of the Chairman of
the Commission, Bishop Guano, who was unfortunately ill.

The document begins by saying how much the Church

wishes to feel herself involved in the affairs of mankind, and how anxious she is to give some help not only to children of the Catholic Church, but to all Christians and, indeed, to all men. The decree recognises the fact that it is the individual who counts, stating that 'it is the human person which must be saved and the human society which must be renewed'. It then starts on an attempt to describe the conditions in which man lives today in this revolutionary era, with vast changes taking place all over the world and with an unprecedented and alarming increase in population with all the problems of poverty and hunger which go with it. It touches also on the problems of youth, the emancipation of women, the desire for liberty and independence in the developing countries, and general un-certainty and anxiety about the future. Against this background the decree talks of the 'Vocation of the Human Person' and of 'The Human Community' and some of the problems which face society, of 'The Significance of Human Activity in the World' and of 'The Rôle of the Church in the World of Today'.

All this was thought to be rather vague and theoretical, and it came in for a good deal of criticism. After a false start by Cardinal Spellman, who raised the question of Conscientious Objection, which would not come up until they reached §101, the debate got going. There was a fairly general feeling that the decree was too long, and that it was repetitive, vague and con-fusing. Some were critical of its theology or of its latinity. A good many thought it would be a terrible anticlimax, and a great disappointment to the world. Yet it had its supporters, among them Archbishop Hermaniuk, of the Ukrainians in Canada, who said that 'despite its weaknesses the text is most promising and may easily prove to be the crown of the entire work of Vatican II'. Many, indeed, hoped that this might be so. But there were doubts.

It was, of course, when the fathers got on to Part II and the practical problems, that the real divisions of opinion began to appear. Here was a lot of inflammable material, some of which aroused sharp debate. Again it was the two problems of Family Planning and Nuclear Warfare – the Pill and the Bomb – which caused most trouble.

On Family Planning the Commission stuck to its guns in saying that the right to determine the number of their children rested with the parents. The text now read as follows:

> 'Married people know that in setting up and running a family they may not be led by their own caprice, but that they must be guided by a conscience rightly formed in accordance with God's law; they know too that it is for them to decide the number of their children in response to God's gifts and to the indications of authentic love.'

This brought a number of comments, from both sides. Some of the fathers thought that any kind of limitation of families was contrary to divine law; others knew that sooner or later something would have to be done, partly to meet the menace of the 'population explosion', and partly to relieve the consciences of what Maximos IV called that 'vast majority of Christian couples' who felt themselves obliged to keep the number of their children within reasonable limits. The position of the Council was extremely difficult. In 1930 Pius XI had condemned any sort of artificial contraception as 'shameful and intrinsically immoral', and had declared that 'any use of matrimony whatsoever in the exercise of which the act is deprived, by human interference, of its natural power to procreate life, is an offence against the law of God and of nature, and those who commit it are guilty of a grave sin'.[1] It would naturally seem strange if, a generation later, the Church were to allow some relaxations in its official teaching. Those who believed most sincerely in the *magisterium* of the Church were naturally worried lest that teaching office should appear to waver.

The question of Peace and War came up for discussion im-

[1] *Casti Connubii*, §54, 56.

mediately after Pope Paul's visit to the United Nations when he had made his great appeal to all men to live in peace. With his words: 'No more war: war never again' ringing in their ears, the fathers settled down to see what they could find to say which would be of help and encouragement to the world. But nothing very striking came out of their cogitations. It was easy enough for Brezanoczy, the auxiliary Bishop of Eger in Hungary, to say that 'the Council should fulminate a solemn, clear, grave and absolute condemnation of nuclear warfare'; but everyone knew that that was impossible. There was also a good deal of talk about 'just wars' and 'unjust wars'; but no one was much impressed by that. All the fathers knew that the main problem was not how to fight a war if it comes, but how to prevent war from breaking out. One of the best speeches on this subject was made by Ottaviani, who gave four ways in which the world should try to remove the causes of war – by more and better education, by promoting international brotherhood without distinction of race or colour, by a fairer distribution of the world's goods, and by a relentless war against totalitarianism in all its forms – which was by far his most constructive contribution to the Council. Archbishop Beck of Liverpool also made a clear and important speech on limitations of sovereignty. But, on the whole, this debate, like so many others which have been staged, ended more or less in an impasse.

One of the subjects which kept cropping up during these days was the problem of the Conscientious Objector, which, as a moral rather than a political problem, was more within the competence of a gathering of theologians and Churchmen. Nothing had been said about Conscientious Objection in the first draft of the decree; but in the second text we read as follows:

'It is not lawful for anyone to give or to carry out orders which are clearly in contrast with God's law, such as the massacre of innocents and prisoners. . . . Furthermore, under present circum-

stances, it would seem fitting for legislation to reflect a positive
attitude towards those people who, as a witness of Christian
gentleness (*lenitas*), or out of respect for human life, or sincere dis-
taste for all use of violence, refuse, in conscience, to do military
service or certain actions which, in time of war, lead to barbarous
cruelty.'

This was an interesting interpolation. In England and some
other countries a man's conscientious scruples against fighting,
even in time of total war, have been respected and protected by
law. But in many countries this is not so, and some moral
theologians felt that a great injustice was being done in forcing
men to do things which their consciences regarded as wrong.
The question had been discussed informally from time to time
during the Council, and Dr Douglas Steere, on behalf of the
Quakers, had made a number of appeals to the fathers to take
up this cause and do justice to the rights of conscience. It was
partly due to his campaigning that this paragraph was now
inserted in the Schema. It did not, of course, suit everybody. We
have already seen that Cardinal Spellman could not contain
his indignation and, long before the debate on Peace and War
had really got started, plunged in with a condemnation of
Conscientious Objection as a sign of disobedience to the Church.
But the English hierarchy were on the side of religious liberty,
Abbot Butler saying that, in his opinion, the Council ought to
accept the fact that duty sometimes compels a man to withhold
obedience even to lawful authority. 'The Conscientious Ob-
jectors', he said, 'are not morally immature. Some of them, in
fact, may really be prophets of a truly Christian morality'.

Apart from the Pill and the Bomb, the debate on Part II of
the Schema did not get very far. There were constant attempts
to get a massive condemnation of atheism (and, therefore, of
Russian Communism); but nothing very much was done. A
good deal of attention was given to world poverty, and several
of the Indian prelates tried to impress upon their colleagues

how terrible conditions were in their part of the world. There was also a good deal of talk about Social Justice, more than one speaker suggesting the setting up of a new Secretariat for Social Justice as one of the Vatican offices. In the midst of all this Bishop Lebrun of Autun gave us his views on sport, and Cardinal Cardijn called on the workers of the world to unite.

After fourteen days of debate on this Schema, it was decided on 8 October, that enough had been said for the Commission to revise it in accordance with the views which had been expressed. On 15 November it came back in its third dress. No more speeches were made (apart from the *relatios*), but fathers were allowed to express their views in the form of a *placet iuxta modum* vote. On each chapter there was a considerable number of modi – 523 on the last one which dealt with Peace and War. So once again the Commission had to get to work in order to produce a text which could be finally accepted and promulgated.

In its final form the Schema on 'The Church in the Modern World' is a very long document of 35,000 words – i.e half the length of this book. Some of it is, to the experienced reader, a bit pedestrian and banal. It hardly needed an assembly of 2,300 prelates from all over the world to tell us that 'the industrial type of society is gradually being spread', or that 'new and more efficient media of social communication are contributing to the knowledge of events'; and most people are already aware of the fact that 'growing numbers of people are abandoning religion in practice'. The whole of the first part, which attempts to describe the conditions in which modern man lives, inevitably falls a bit flat. It has all been said so many times before. When I first read the Schema I expressed my feelings of disappointment to one of the periti. His reply was rather surprising: 'Of course it is disappointing to you,' he said, 'because Anglicans have been interested in Christian Sociology for years, at any rate since the days of Frederick Denison Maurice and the Christian Socialists;

but you must remember that all this sort of thing is totally new to large numbers of Catholic bishops, especially from some of the more reactionary countries'. That is true; and it was, no doubt, necessary to teach them in fairly simple language what they were being asked to vote on.

At the same time, a good many of the Council fathers had doubts as to whether a document of this kind was really appropriate to an ecumenical Council. Most people would agree with Suenens and others, that people were looking to the Council for help in the everyday problems which they had to face; but should this be given in the form of a conciliar 'constitution'? Some thought it would have been better to have addressed the world in the form of a pastoral letter, and it was as a result of their suggestions that the document was finally described as a 'Pastoral Constitution'. But some of the Council fathers were still unhappy about it.

If Part I of the Constitution tries to say too much, there was a general feeling that Part II had not said enough. On the real controversial matters the Council had failed to give a clear lead, for the simple reason that the fathers were as much divided on some of these issues as the world outside. This is always true. 'Why doesn't the Church give us a lead?' people impatiently ask. And the answer is because those who speak on behalf of the Church are as fallible and as divided as anyone else. This was particularly noticeable when the Council got on to the subjects of Contraception and Nuclear War.

On the first of these the final text says that parents, in determining the number of children which they wish to have must 'thoughtfully take into account both their own welfare and that of their children, those already born and those which the future may bring. For this accounting they need to reckon with both the material and the spiritual conditions of the times as well as of their state in life. Finally they should consult the interests of the family group, of temporal society and of the

Church herself. The parents themselves should ultimately make this judgment in the sight of God' (§ 50). Then, after talking of the duty to procreate, the text says that parents 'may find themselves in circumstances where at least temporarily the size of the families should not be increased'; but, of course, nothing is said about the ways in which this limitation may be effected. This was, no doubt, deliberately left vague so as not to appear to be contradicting the very forcible teaching of Pius XI in 'Casti connubii'. But later on (in § 87) the text refers again to birth control when dealing with the urgent problem of the rapid increase in population. Here it says that 'men should judiciously be informed of scientific advances in exploring methods whereby spouses can be helped in regulating the number of their children, and whose safeness has been well proven, and whose harmony with the moral order has been ascertained'. 'Scientific advances' must mean something more than confining intercourse to what is known as the 'safe period'; but the text deliberately leaves things vague, partly because the fathers were finding it very difficult to decide what was 'in harmony with the moral order' and what was not, and partly because it was known that the Pope was appointing a fairly large commission to consider the whole problem from a theological, moral, medical and psychological point of view.

On the question of Nuclear War the text is more outspoken. 'Actions', it says, 'designed for the methodical extermination of an entire people, nation or ethnic minority . . . must be vehemently condemned as terrible crimes'; and again: 'Any act of war aimed indiscriminately at the destruction of entire cities or extensive areas along with their population is a crime against God and man himself. It merits unequivocal and unhesitating condemnation' (§ 79–80). It also has a good deal of useful stuff to say about the evils of the 'arms race' and the importance of seeking to destroy or remove the causes of war. But with the Americans fighting in Vietnam, India and Pakistan at war with each other, and many nations strengthening their military power by whatever means were available (including nuclear weapons), it would have looked hypocritical for the Council to have condemned all war as evil. The fathers were, in this, wiser than their Anglican brethren who, in 1930, solemnly declared that 'war as a method of settling international disputes is incompatible with the teaching and example of our Lord Jesus Christ',[1] and nine years later were backing up the Government in its effort to crush Hitler's Germany.

The Council fathers had, indeed, to walk warily. If they had condemned the piling up of armaments, they would have made things more difficult for the faithful in the satellite and occupied countries. Their constitution is, therefore, inevitably disappointing to those who were demanding a 'clear lead'. Perhaps it would have been better not to have attempted a task of this delicacy and magnitude; but, once they had started out on it, they clearly could not turn back. The final text will not solve the world's problems, but it may help to make people think more deeply about them; and, if it does that, it will have achieved something.

Once they had got 'Religious Liberty' and 'The Church in the Modern World' out of the way, there was not very much more for the Council to do. Only two texts needed any debate, one on Missionary Activity and the other on Priestly Life; for the rest, it was a question of the Commissons working as hard as they could on written observations and on modi in order to present a text which the fathers as a whole would be prepared to accept.

Of the two Schemata which needed further discussion something has already been said of the final stages of the decree on Missionary Activity.[2] That on Priestly Life and Ministry had fared very badly in 1964, when the fathers had more or less

---

[1] *Lambeth Conferences (1867–1930)* (London, 1948), p. 168.
[2] See above, pp. 123–5.

thrown it out as unworthy of its theme, and the Commission had had to prepare something better. In its new form the Schema was obviously a great improvement on the very sketchy document which had been rejected. Naturally it referred back to the great Constitution *De Ecclesia* for its theological basis; but *De Ecclesia* had given only one paragraph to the priesthood (as against ten for the bishops), and the Council felt that the priests deserved something better than this in view of the excellent work which they were doing in all parts of the world.

The Schema starts off by saying that every priest shares in the ministry of Christ as Teacher, Priest and King. It then develops this theme, pointing out that, as Teacher, the priest must prepare himself by study and meditation in order to be a true minister of the Word; that, as Priest, he must duly administer the Sacraments, and especially the Eucharist; and that, as King, he must guide and govern the people committed to his charge. It then goes on to consider the priest in relation to the episcopate, to his fellow priests and to the laity. In each section the priesthood is shown to be an office of great dignity and importance in the mission of the Church, and one which demands the utmost devotion and loyalty. After dealing with the distribution of priests in the world, the Schema naturally leads on to the subject of vocation and the need to attract good men to the ministry, from which it goes on to discuss the self-giving required in obedience, celibacy and poverty, and ends with some practical details.

In the debate on this, Cardinal Arriba y Castro said that he regarded this as the most important Schema which the Council had to consider, and a good many of the bishops agreed with him. They knew that the health and well-being of the Church depended very largely on the priesthood. If the clergy were devoted and hard-working men, then the mission of the Church had some chance of going forward; but, if the clergy were idle or worldly, then stagnation must inevitably ensue. A lot, therefore, was said about the priest's spiritual life and also about his pastoral duties and care for his people. The whole tone of the discussion was one of concern for men, some of whom were working in difficult and discouraging circumstances and who needed all the help and support which the Council could give them.

After this discussion the Council was mostly concerned with voting on the texts as they were produced for them by the various Commissions. On 28 October a general session was held, at which five decrees were solemnly promulgated – those on 'The Pastoral Office of Bishops in the Church', 'Priestly Training', 'Adaptation and Renewal of the Religious Life', 'Christian Education' and 'The Relation of the Church to Non-Christian Religions'. On the following day the Council polished off the constitution on 'Divine Revelation', and than had ten days' holiday to allow the Commissions to catch up a bit. The next congregation was on 9 November, after which the fathers met pretty regularly until the 19th when there was another gap of ten days before the four last gatherings.

During these last few weeks there was little debate. The time for that had passed, for the Pope had told the world that this was to be the last session of the Council, and a lot of work had to be got through behind the scenes if the Schemata were to be finally accepted. Day after day, therefore, passed when the only business before the Council was to vote on the various documents which the Vatican Polyglot Press was busily turning out in its immaculate type.

In order to fill in the time, a document on the subject of Indulgences was laid before the Council on 9 November for its consideration. It appears that, when the bishops were asked, way back in 1961, what subjects they wished the Council to discusss, a good many of them asked for a decree on Indulgences. This was rejected by the Preparatory Commission; but a group of canonists was asked to produce a document laying down the 'norms' on which any changes in Canon Law on this subject might be considered. The statement which they produced dealt with four matters. One was 'partial indulgences' (that is, indulgences limited to a specific number of days or years); another was 'plenary indulgences', which they thought needed to be limited; the third was concerned with new rules for attaching indulgences to objects of piety where the danger of superstition is obvious; and the fourth dealt with 'privileged altars'.

This document was meant to be a sign of reform, an indication that the Church was prepared to revise its practice in giving indulgences, bringing it more into line with modern thought. But it was not so regarded by many of the Council fathers. Maximos IV started off with a devastating attack on the whole thing. He pointed out that indulgences of this kind had no place in the life of the Eastern Churches, that they belonged to an ancient penitential discipline which had long since disappeared, that they were based on a totally wrong conception of God's mercy, and that the document now before the Council would seriously affect the better relations which now existed between Rome and the rest of Christendom. After this, each episcopal conference, or local hierarchy, was asked to give its views. Cardinal Shehan of Baltimore spoke on behalf of the United States hierarchy and surprised everyone by saying that his colleagues were in favour of the document, though doubtful whether the time was ripe for it.[1] Wyszynski, on behalf of the Poles, supported it whole-heartedly; but first Alfrink, and then König and Doepfner, declared in the strongest way that this statement was theologically unsound and ecumenically disastrous. On the following day we expected further contributions; but nothing was said, and the whole subject was quietly dropped. Rumour had it that the next report was to come from the Canadian bishops, and that it was so shattering in

---

[1] It must, however, be pointed out that he had consulted less than half of the American bishops – 116 out of 244.

its criticisms that the Secretary General thought it wisest to close the debate.

On 18 November another public session was held at which two more texts were finally passed and duly promulgated, one on 'Divine Revelation', the other on the 'Lay Apostolate'. On this occasion the Pope made a speech of some significance, in which he declared his intention of doing four things. One was to reform the Curia, another to set in motion the machinery for the canonization of his two predecessors – Pius XII and John XXIII – another was to build in Rome a church to be dedicated to Mary, Mother of the Church, and the last to declare a Jubilee. All of these proposals were met with loud and prolonged applause, especially that which referred to the proposed canonizations, though we liked to think that the acclamations were directed to Pope John rather than to Pope Pius. The announcement of a six-month Jubilee caused a certain amount of irritation to the observers, especially the passage in the text which declared freedom from censure and ecclesiastical punishment during that time for those who 'read or possess books written by apostates, heretics and schismatics'. We thought this might easily have been omitted in view of the fact that several of the conciliar decrees had encouraged the faithful to learn more about those who were now politely called 'separated brethren', but who would obviously officially come under the heading of 'schismatics', if not something worse.

After this we had five more sittings, in which the remaining texts were voted on, and the Council came to an end. By this time people were getting weary of the whole thing. Apart from the short discussion on indulgences, there had been little of interest going on for more than a month, and time had dragged while votes were being counted and there was nothing to do except talk and drink coffee to the background of local choral societies singing Palestrina.

There were, however, three big services which gave life to the

Council in its final stages. The first was the joint Service in S. Paul's-without-the-Walls on 4 December, to which reference has already been made.[1] The second was the last public session in S. Peter's three days later when the remaining four decrees – on 'Religious Liberty', 'Missionary Activity', 'Priestly Life and Ministry' and 'The Church in the Modern World' – were finally passed and promulgated. Once again the observers had the seats of honour in front of the tribune of S. Longinus with every opportunity to observe what was taking place. Some of us found these occasions very impressive – full of colour, dignity, ceremonial and joy. But not all of the observers felt like this. Some found them very distasteful, as if they emphasised all that they most disliked in Roman Catholicism – arrogance, triumphalism, display, worldliness and self-assurance. On this occasion I noticed that, although we were all supplied with exquisitely printed copies of the service, some of the observers took no part in it, not even joining in the Lord's Prayer. Some seemed to regard these great services principally as opportunities for taking photographs, though in this they were by no means alone, for many of the bishops had ciné-cameras going during the service, and I saw, immediately behind the Pope, a little group of nuns who, at the Elevation of the Host (the most solemn moment in the liturgy, when anyone who believes in the Real Presence would wish to kneel down and adore), were busily taking flashlight photographs of what was going on.

In many ways the most moving and significant incident in this service was the lifting of the anathemas and excommunications which had been imposed at the time of the breach between East and West in 1054. This was done by a Joint Statement, signed by Pope Paul and the Ecumenical Patriarch Athenagoras, which declared that

'(a) they regret the offensive words, the reproaches without foundation, and the reprehensible gestures which, on both

[1] See above, pp. 30–31.

sides, have marked or accompanied the sad events of this
period;

'(b) they likewise regret and remove from memory and from the
midst of the Church the sentences of excommunication which
followed these events . . . and commit these excommunications to oblivion;

'(c) they deplore the preceding and later events which, under the
influence of various factors, among which lack of understanding and mutual trust eventually led to the effective
rupture of ecclesiastical communion.'

After this had been read, Metropolitan Meliton of Heliopolis
made a dignified entry and, amid immense applause, walked up
to the platform to be embraced by the Pope. This was, of course,
no more than a gesture, an attempt to wipe out old scores and
promote better understanding and charity; but it seemed a
stepping-stone on the way to a possible union of the two churches
at some future date. Some of us wondered whether the day
would come when a similar ceremony might be conducted in
which the excommunication and dethronement of Elizabeth I
by Pius V in 1570 might also be 'committed to oblivion'.

On 8 December, the Feast of the Immaculate Conception, an
open-air service on the steps of S. Peter's was planned. Those of
us who came from countries where it is dangerous to plan open-
air services in June wondered at the audacity of those who
could imagine it would be fine and warm enough to hold such
a service in December. But they were justified. Although
chilly, it did not rain; and bishops from the tropics managed to
survive the rigours of sitting for three hours in the open air by
wearing thick jerseys under their episcopal robes. After the
Mass and the closing ceremonies, messages were sent by the
Pope to various categories – Rulers, Men of Thought and
Science, Artists, Women, Workers, Sick and Poor, and Youth.
As each message was read out three people representing that
group went up to receive it, amid loud applause from the tens
of thousands gathered in the piazza.

So ended the twenty-first general Council, the last of a series which began in 325 when the Church was rejoicing in its new-found freedom after three centuries of inhibition and persecution. Now some forty per cent of mankind profess the Christian faith, men 'of all nations, and kindreds, and peoples and tongues'. But only half the Christian population was represented at the Vatican Council, for the Church, which has so often been likened to the seamless robe of Christ, has been divided into many pieces, of different sizes and shapes. That the disciples of Christ should be so divided is a grief which we all have to bear. The question which many of us were asking, as we walked away from S. Peter's on that December morning was: What will this Council have done towards the healing of those divisions?

CHAPTER SEVEN

So What?

TO HAVE SAT THROUGH THE BEST PART OF FOUR
sessions of an Ecumenical Council has been a remarkable experience. To those of us interested in Church History, it has
been thrilling to sit in the observers' box and watch history being
made before our eyes. For there can be no doubt that this
Second Vatican Council will, in future, be regarded as one of
the turning-points in the history of the Christian Church, not
only of the Church of Rome.

The Council has undoubtedly done a great deal for the
Roman Catholic Church. For the first time in their lives the
bishops have been brought together from all over the world, to
meet, discuss, argue, fraternise and finally legislate for the whole
Church. To bishops from small dioceses in the mission-field the
mere size of the gathering must have been impressive. They
must have felt, as never before, the universality of the Church, as
bishops of every colour and from almost every country sat side
by side in the great nave of S. Peter's day by day to discuss their
problems and thrash out the policy of the Church.

The sense of solidarity which the Council conveyed was mixed
with a sense of variety. Not only did the bishops differ from one
another in colour, race and language; they also differed very
much in their opinions. The Council, in fact, produced a great

collision between two opposing forces, the force of reform and renewal and the force of conservatism and complacency.

Many of the bishops came from countries where the Church of Rome was dominant, powerful, ubiquitous. They accepted the fact that there was room for reform, for the Church is always in need of that; but it should not be such as to change the image of the Church or weaken the power of the priesthood. As for Ecumenism, many of them were naturally unfamiliar with the subject. Bishops in Calabria or Sicily, for example, had probably never met a Protestant, and therefore knew little about the non-Roman forms of Christianity apart from the negative and censorious things which they had read in pious manuals. Others had seen something of the non-Roman world, and what they had seen they had found disagreeable. There was, therefore, a large, and, to some extent, powerful body among the bishops which wanted the Council to show the world how splendid the Church of Rome is – how big, how wise, how holy. If the Council did this, then it would do a good work. But beware lest the Council should undermine the power of the papacy, or the curia, or the bishops or the priesthood. Above all things, let the Council beware of giving the impression that the Church was wavering in its belief that it, and it alone, was the Church founded by Christ, outside which there can be no salvation.

Meanwhile there was a considerable number of bishops, mostly from the more enlightened countries, who saw the Council as the opportunity for which they had long been waiting. They knew that, if the Church was to go forward in the work of evangelising the world, big reforms were necessary. They believed that the power of the curia must be limited, that there must be more local independence so that the Church can adapt itself to the needs of the day, that old ways of teaching the faith must be reformed as must also old ways of worshipping God. They were faced, many of them, with diminishing numbers of clergy and of laity and with the charge that the Church was out of touch with the modern world. They were determined, therefore, to make this a Council of reform, of renewal, of readjustment. They were also aware of the problems of Christian division, and some of them were ashamed that the Roman Catholic Church had been so independent and had, in the past, given so little help to the cause of Christian Unity. They wanted, therefore, to make this an 'ecumenical' Council in more senses than one, hoping that, out of it, would come closer co-operation and understanding between the Roman and non-Roman world.

As a result of the great collision which we saw taking place in S. Peter's, the whole ecumenical pattern has changed. It is true, of course, that the Council had to limit itself to laying down certain principles; and it will be the Church's task during the next few years to show how these principles can be worked out. But the decrees are there for all to see and to appeal to, expressions of the Church's position with regard to many different subjects – the Bible, dogma, ministry, worship, primacy, mission, and so on. The Council has shaken the Roman Catholic Church out of its complacency and isolation, and has brought it face to face not only with itself but also with the rest of Christendom, and, to some extent, with the world.

But if the Council has forced the Church of Rome to look at things from a new angle, it must also affect Christians of other allegiances and require them to look again at the problem of Christian Unity. The 'given unity', shared by all who accept Christ as Lord and Saviour, makes it inevitable that whatever happens in one part of the Body of Christ is bound to be felt in every other part. The result of the Council, therefore, has been to alter the whole ecumenical pattern and to carry the ecumenical discussion into a new field. Up to 1962 the idea of unity, in which *all* who profess the Christian faith could become in any real sense *one*, appeared so remote as to be scarcely worthy of consideration by rational minds. Rome was isolated and aloof, and there seemed little prospect of her ever being otherwise. Non-Roman Christians were, therefore, obliged to go their own way and try to reach such limited unity as appeared to be possible.

But now things look different. Rome has, at last, begun to interest herself in the problem of Unity, and things can never be the same again. John XXIII had expressed the desire that the Council should do something for Christian Unity, and the ecumenical urge was felt all through its deliberations. Whatever subject was under consideration, the thought of how it would affect other Christians was never far away. The sensitivity of the Council towards the feelings and convictions of others was one of the things which most impressed itself upon the observers.

In the Constitution on the Church a whole paragraph is concerned with 'the status of separated Christians' and opens with the words: 'The Church recognises that in many ways she is linked with those who, being baptised, are honoured with the name of Christian.' In the decree which describes the work of the bishops we read that 'they should deal lovingly with the separated brethren, urging the faithful also to conduct themselves with great kindness and charity in their regard and fostering ecumenism as it is understood by the Church'. The decree on the priesthood says that 'following the example of the Good Shepherd . . . and taking note of the regulations about Ecumenism, they must not forget the brethren who do not enjoy full ecclesiastical communion with us'. On the training of men for the priesthood, the decree states that 'students must be brought to a full understanding of the Churches and ecclesial communities separated from the Apostolic Roman See, so that they may be able to contribute to the work of re-establishing unity among all Christians according to the prescriptions of this Holy Synod'. And in the decree on the Apostolate of the Laity we read that 'the common heritage, so to speak, of the Gospel, and the common duty of Christian witness resulting from it,

recommend and frequently require the co-operation of Catholics with other Christians on the part of individuals and
communities within the Church, either in activities or in
associations, in the national or international field'. No one
could read through the whole set of the Council decrees without
realising how close is the ecumenical significance of what is
being said. In this the Council was faithful to the wishes of
Pope John.

At the same time we must not fall into the mistake of being
over-optimistic. In spite of what the Council has done, the
problem of Christian Unity remains very stubborn and difficult.
The Council has not, in fact, solved any part of that problem.
What it has done is to enable Christians to look at the problem
in a new light and in a new atmosphere. We can now begin to
look at the problem together, conscious of a mutual desire to
find some solution and, in the meanwhile, to avoid recrimina-
tion and hostility.

But if we must beware of too much optimism, we must beware also of over-pessimism. There are many who will tell us
that the Council has really done nothing; that courtesy and
friendliness are no substitute for changes in dogma; that Rome
is as adamant as ever in demanding unconditional surrender.
There are also those, on the other side, who will say that any
kind of union between Rome and Protestantism is impossible so
long as Protestants continue to regard Rome as Babylon and the
Pope as anti-Christ; that Catholicism and Protestantism are
irreconcilable; that many outside the Roman Church are so
invincibly ignorant that there is no hope of converting them.
Subsidiary to mutual feelings of pessimism and hopelessness is
the reluctance to make the effort to go forward. In some parts
of the world this is particularly true, countries in which antagon-
ism and rivalry have become so deep-seated that it is hard to
see any prospect of their eradication.

Meanwhile, between the poles of optimism and pessimism

lies the course of realism. The Council has, as it were, opened
a number of doors. We may not be willing as yet to go through
them; but at least we should try to keep them open, and perhaps
take the opportunity of looking through them to see what it is
like on the other side. By so doing we shall learn a lot about
each other and shall probably discover (perhaps to our surprise)
that the things which unite us are infinitely bigger and more
important than the things which divide us. In a world in which
the cause of Christ is fighting for its existence, where non-
Christian forces are powerful and determined, where Christians
of all kinds are falling by the wayside, where materialism is
rampant and the danger of self-destruction imminent, the
Christian force cannot afford the luxury of division. Each type
of Christianity has something to offer to the needs of the world.
Is there no way in which we can ensure that all the resources
and wealth of Christian faith and hope are made available towards the healing of the world's sickness?

The Council has done much to stimulate the determination of
all Christians to work for unity. It has created a new 'sense of
unity', a feeling of common concern for the world's needs and
for the cause of Christ, a feeling in which all can now share. We
know that we are all in this together, and that no Church can
feel complacent either about the progress of the Gospel or about
its own spiritual health. No Church is making much progress
today. Figures of converts are published from time to time; but
no one can record the number of the lapsed, the people who
have drifted away from any church allegiance. In face of this
'wasting sickness', it is essential that Christian forces should try
to act together.

The Council has done much to stimulate a desire for co-
operation. How co-operation can take place, and what form or
forms it may assume, are questions which we cannot immediately answer. Perhaps the principle laid down by the Faith and
Order conference at Lund in 1952 – that Churches should ask

G

themselves 'whether they should not act together in all matters except those in which deep differences of conviction compel them to act separately'[1] – is as good a starting-point as any. If we gave some serious thought to this we might find that the matters in which we are compelled 'to act separately' are not as great as they sometimes appear, blurred and hidden in the fog of ignorance, suspicion, jealousy and fear.

When I say 'we' I am naturally thinking of the Anglican Church, to which I belong. I am often asked what the Council thought about the Anglican Church, whereupon I have to reply that, to a large number of the Council fathers, the Anglican Church was practically unknown. Of the 2,300 members, 385 were Italian bishops, 227 came from Brazil, 85 from Spain and 74 from Mexico. None of these could be expected to know much about a Church which had practically no existence in their country, and yet these four groups together formed more than one-third of the whole Council.

In English-speaking countries, and in the mission-field, Roman Catholics had come more into contact with Anglicans, and some of the bishops from these countries were pretty well-informed about the Christians among whom they lived. Some of them found Anglicanism unattractive and difficult to understand. They were shocked at the lack of discipline. They felt bound to disapprove of a Church which has so many of the marks of true Catholicism – episcopacy, priesthood, liturgy, sacraments, etc. – and yet refuses the one essential thing – submission to the authority of the See of Rome. They knew that their Church had condemned Anglican orders as invalid, thereby denying validity to any sacraments performed by their clergy. In fact, the whole thing appeared to some of them as slightly bogus, a pretence, an aping of Catholicism which was worse than good, downright Protestantism.

[1] G. K. A. Bell, *Documents on Christian Unity: Fourth Series*, p. 224.

Others, however, were intrigued by Anglicanism. In a way they could see in it many of the things for which they were working – a reformed liturgy, greater emphasis on Bible-study, married clergy, lay participation in the government of the Church and so on. These were men who were not bogged down by history, who could see a mediaeval church without thinking that it had been stolen from them, who could look upon Anglicans not as rivals or usurpers but as a form of Christian life worthy of consideration.

It was from men of this type that the remarkable statement was put into the decree on Ecumenism declaring that 'among those [Churches] in which Catholic traditions and institutions in part continue to exist, the Anglican Communion occupies a special place'. At first sight it seems strange that the Council should have gone out of its way to mention any one of the many Churches and communities which are said to have 'stemmed from the events which are commonly referred to as the Reformation'. No other Church of East or West is mentioned by name. No reason is given as to why the Anglican Communion is singled out in this way. Nor is it known where the phrase originated, or who suggested that it should be inserted in the text of a conciliar decree. One or two bishops referred to the Anglican Communion when the decree on Ecumenism was being debated, and it was, presumably, on the basis of this that the Secretariat for Unity, who prepared the draft, decided to insert this phrase.

Relations between the Secretariat for Unity and the Anglican Church have been cordial ever since the Secretariat was founded in 1960. These relations were strengthened by the courageous and imaginative action of Lord Fisher, then Archbishop of Canterbury, in paying a courtesy visit to Pope John in 1960. This was followed early in the following year by the appointment of Canon Bernard Pawley as an unofficial representative of the Archbishops of Canterbury and York, to

live in Rome and 'keep their Graces informed of the progress o
the preparations for the Council, especially as far as they migh
have any bearing on the future of the relations between the twc
Churches, and to be at the disposal of the Secretariat for Unity
by way of supplying information or answers to questions concerning the beliefs and practices of the Church of England'.
For eighteen months before the Council met, Canon Pawley
was steadily building up good relations with the Secretariat
and indeed with Pope John and many of the Vatican officials
all of which have borne good fruit in subsequent years.

When the invitation to send observers to the Council reached
Lambeth Palace, Archbishop Ramsey acted without delay, and
a team was immediately appointed. In addition to the three
official observers we had also the great advantage of having
Canon Pawley, and later Canon Findlow, as a 'guest' of the
Council, and were joined by one or two other Anglicans such
as Bishop Sadiq of Nagpur representing the World Council o
Churches in 1963, the Reverend William Norgren of the
National Council of Churches of Christ in the U.S.A. in 1963-
65, and the Reverend Frank Cuttriss of the Australian Counci
of Churches for the last session. Unlike some observers, most o
the Anglicans stayed for considerable periods and so became
integrated into the life and work of the Council. We acted very
much as a team, met regularly to discuss policy, entertained
prominent members of the Council,[2] organised receptions, and
were, I think, the only denominational group to be given a
private audience by the Pope.

It was no doubt from this, and from the remarks of certain
bishops in the Council, that the Anglican Communion wa
accorded this 'special place' in the decree on Ecumenism. Wha

---

[1] B. C. Pawley, *Looking at the Vatican Council* (London, 1962), p. 18.

[2] Paul VI (as Cardinal Montini) and at least twenty-one other Cardinal
found their way at some time or other to the Anglican headquarters in th
Via Napoli.

precisely is meant by this phrase is not made clear; but presumably the bishops were prepared to recognise the fact that, compared with other 'churches and ecclesial communities' in the West which have moved a long way from the mediaeval Church, and have thereby broken with many Catholic traditions and demolished many Catholic institutions, the Anglican Church was preserved so much from the past, and is therefore closer than any other communion to the Church of Rome.

This statement might be challenged by those who are particularly conscious of the protestant and reformed nature of the Anglican Church; but if one compares the teaching and practice of the Church of England with that of Presbyterianism or Congregationalism, one will see how great the difference is. There is, as we all know, much variety in the Anglican Church; but if one wants to know what the Church stands for one must look, not at the work of individual writers, nor at what goes on in individual churches, but at the official and semi-official declarations which carry some authority – the Prayer Book, the Articles of Religion, such Canons as exist, Acts of Convocation and Church Assembly measures, and, to some extent, the reports of Lambeth Conferences. The fact that Bishops Barnes or Bishop Robinson have written works of doubtful orthodoxy, or that some clergyman has said he doesn't believe in the Virgin Birth, or that some parish churches offer what is called 'open Communion' or write their own forms of service, are problems not of theology but of discipline. The Anglican Church is weak in discipline, but its theological basis is fairly easy to discover.

The decree on Ecumenism speaks of the 'traditions and institutions (*structurae*)' for which the Anglican Church is notable. These would include such things as a clear doctrine of the Church; the preservation of the three-fold ministry of bishops, priests and deacons; emphasis on the sacraments, with six out of the seven provided for in the Book of Common Prayer; a fixed liturgy based very largely on pre-Reformation forms; a liturgical year which includes, among other things, five feasts of the Blessed Virgin; the continuation of the administrative structure of province, diocese, archdeaconry, deanery and parish; and the fact that the religious life has been restored during the last hundred years or so.

It was no doubt on the basis of all this, and of the fact that Romans and Anglicans use the same phraseology, call things by the same names and have so much in common, that the statement about the 'special place' was put into the decree. And, having made this statement, the Roman Catholic Church is naturally anxious to follow it up. Pope Paul takes a great interest in the Anglican Church and often asks for further information about it. He was for a long time anxious to receive the Archbishop of Canterbury, and on several occasions asked me whether I thought he would come. I assured him that he would, and later had the pleasure of accompanying the Archbishop on his memorable visit to Rome in March 1966 when he was received with the utmost courtesy and honour. Never before had the leader of any Church not in communion with Rome received anything like the attention which was given to the Archbishop on this occasion, when he was solemnly received in the Sistine Chapel, and when the two leaders joined in a great service of thanksgiving and prayer in the basilica of S. Paul's-without-the-walls. As a result of the decree on Ecumenism, and of subsequent events, the Anglican Communion is now establishing an Anglican Centre in Rome with a library of Anglican history and theology for the use of students and enquirers, and with adequate rooms for lectures, discussions and social gatherings. Meanwhile, the Pope and the Archbishop have issued a joint statement promising the establishment of a Commission to study and discuss the problems which keep us apart.

In this atmosphere of cordiality and courtesy there is, perhaps, a danger of our forgetting, or minimising, the very real problems which still stand in the way of any union between Canterbury and Rome. These fall, roughly, under four headings. There is, first of all, the problem of ecclesiology. Anglicans are confident that the Church to which they belong is the true Church, founded by Christ and developed and extended by the apostles. While being positive about this, they try not to be negative about other Christians. Few Anglicans would doubt that Roman Catholics and Orthodox are also members of the true Church, though some might be a little uncertain about members of the non-episcopal Churches, though without wishing to be dogmatic or exclusive. But with Rome it is different. She has over and over again declared that there is only one true Church, and that is the Church which is in communion with the Roman see. During the course of the Council she has, however, given further thought to the question of imperfect and incomplete membership of the Church being accorded to those who are validly baptised. Two sentences in the Constitution on the Church raise this question. One (§ 10) says: 'the baptised, by the regeneration and anointing of the Holy Spirit, are consecrated as a spiritual house and a holy priesthood, in order that, through all the works of a Christian man, they may offer spiritual sacrifices and proclaim the power of him who has called them out of darkness into his marvellous light'. Another (§ 15) says: 'The Church recognises that in many ways she is linked with those who, being baptised, are honoured with the name of Christ, but do not profess the faith in its entirety or do not preserve unity of communion with the successor of Peter.' Meanwhile the decree on Ecumenism says (§ 3) that 'men who believe in Christ, and have been properly baptised, are brought into a certain, though imperfect, communion with the Catholic Church'; and that 'all who have been justified by faith in baptism are incorporated into Christ, and have, therefore, a right to be called Christians, and with good reason are accepted as brothers by the children of the Catholic Church'. If they are accepted as brothers then, logically, they must also be children of the Catholic Church.

Apart from proclaiming the unity of the baptised, the Council has also expressed a sense of oneness with non-Roman Catholics in another way. In § 8 of the Constitution on the Church we read: 'The one Church of Christ . . . constituted and organised in the world as a society, subsists in the Catholic Church, which is governed by the successor of Peter and by the bishops in communion, although many elements of sanctification and of truth may be found outside its visible structure, which, as gifts belonging to the Church of Christ, are forces impelling towards catholic unity.' On this Fr Gregory Baum writes as follows: 'Instead of simply identifying the Church of Christ with the Catholic Church, the Constitution rather says more carefully that the Church of Christ "subsists in" the Catholic Church. The body of Christ is present in the Catholic Church, but, at the same time, without losing its historical and incarnate character, transcends it. . . . According to Catholic faith, only the Catholic Church perfectly embodies the Church of Christ on earth, but, because of the transcendence of Christ's Church, this does not preclude the possibility that there may be partial realisations of this Church among men.'[1]

The Council has, therefore, admitted that the Church of Christ is something bigger than the Roman Catholic Church. She has also accorded to the Anglican Communion a special place among the non-Roman parts of Christ's Church. Put these two statements together and we have a starting-point for the dialogue which must now take place. Let this dialogue be carried out dispassionately, rationally and free from prejudice or bitterness.

The second problem which will have to be discussed is that

[1] *De Ecclesia: the Constitution on the Church of Vatican Council II*, with commentary by Gregory Baum, O.S.A. (London, 1965), p. 24.

of the Ministry. What we believe about the ministry will clearly depend upon what we believe about the Church. If Roman Catholics were obliged to believe that the Anglican Communion is no part of the Church of Christ, then clearly its orders could have no validity. But if the Anglican Communion is a 'partial realisation' of Christ's Church, then at least we have a basis for discussion of its ministry. Any such discussion will, of course, have to take place against the background of the decree of Leo XIII in 1896 which declared that 'ordinations performed according to the Anglican rite are utterly invalid and altogether void'. So long as this stands unrepealed and unexplained, all Anglican bishops and priests are, in the eyes of the Roman Church, laymen. Courtesy and politeness may persuade Roman Catholics to behave as if things were otherwise – witness the scenes in the Sistine Chapel and S. Paul's basilica on 23 and 24 March, 1966 – but this merely disguises what they believe to be the truth. As I looked at the twenty-seven cardinals sitting before the Pope and the Archbishop on the second of these occasions, I wondered very much what they were thinking.

This question of ministry is always the main stumbling-block in any ecumenical discussion. In most of the schemes and plans which have been drawn up some form of 'Service of Reconciliation' is devised, with the intention of producing a ministry which can be accepted as 'valid' by both sides. This is generally done by means of a formula which is often deliberately left ambiguous so that no one's feelings will be hurt. I doubt whether anything of this kind would satisfy Roman Catholic theologians and canonists, and some other method would have to be devised. This might take the form of conditional ordination, or mutual ordination, or perhaps allowing Roman Catholic bishops to take part in consecrations of Anglican bishops. But all this belongs to the world of conjecture. What we need to do now is to try to reach some agreement on the nature and constituent parts of the Church. Until we have done that, no discussion on the validity of Anglican orders is likely to make much progress.

The third great problem is that of the Papacy. This is one of the chief obstacles on the road towards Christian Unity; but Vatican II has done something towards making it look a little less formidable. At the time of the enormous disaster of 1870, when the First Vatican Council accepted the dogma of Papal Infallibility, the breach between Rome and the rest of Christendom was greatly widened. But in 1965 the Second Vatican Council, by its statements on Collegiality, did something to undo the harm which had been done. We can begin now to see that infallibility is really only a way of saying that there exists a final authority to which man can turn for resolution of his doubts and anxieties. Many people find that they need some such ultimate authority. Some find it in the Bible; some in personal contact with God and the direction which comes to them through prayer and meditation; some find it in the magisterium of the Church. In 1870 Vatican I set up the Pope as this ultimate authority though, in fact, only one 'infallible' statement has been made, and it is now unlikely that there will ever be another. Papal infallibility, therefore, is little more than an academic question. In practice, it means virtually nothing. In the documents emanating from Vatican II the doctrine of Papal Infallibility is assumed. In § 18 of the Constitution on the Church we read that Christ 'placed blessed Peter over the other apostles, and instituted in him a permanent and visible source and foundation of unity of faith and communion. This teaching (it continues) about the institution, the perpetuity, the meaning and reason for the sacred primacy of the Roman pontiff and of his infallible magisterium, this sacred Council again proposes to be firmly believed by all the faithful'. But it then goes on to say that the government and guidance of the Church belongs really to the whole apostolic college. 'In virtue of his office as vicar of Christ and pastor of the whole Church' it says, 'the Roman pontiff has full, supreme and universal power over the Church, and he is always free to exercise this power.' But 'the order of bishops, which succeeds to the college of apostles in teaching and ruling the Church, and which gives this apostolic body continued existence, is also the subject of supreme and full power over the universal Church, together with its head, the Roman pontiff, and never without this head' (§ 22). This is intended to suggest that infallibility is not something which the Pope enjoys alone, but something which he shares with the universal episcopate. This is stated again a little later (§ 25) where we read: 'Although individual bishops do not enjoy the prerogative of infallibility, they nevertheless proclaim Christ's doctrine infallibly, whenever, even though dispersed throughout the world (but still maintaining the bond of communion among themselves and with the successor of Peter, and authentically teaching matters of faith and morals), they are in agreement on one position as definitely to be held.'

All this should take away some of the misunderstanding which has gathered around the doctrine of the Infallibility of the Pope. It has also done something to control the universal jurisdiction of the papacy. This also has been a stumbling-block to mutual understanding between Rome and the rest of Christendom, for the power of the Curia has been strong, reaching to the farthest corners of the earth and affecting the life of every member of the Church. This is something which non-Romans would find very difficult to accept. But there are two factors which ought to be considered. One is that the Council has limited the power of the Curia by insisting that more and more authority should be transferred from Rome to the local hierarchies who alone can know what is needed, and how best the Church can fulfil its mission. The other is that considerable parts of the Church which are in communion with Rome already have a certain degree of independence. These are the Uniat Churches which have their own customs and liturgy, and, in many ways, have far more in common with the 'separated brethren' among whom they live than they have with their fellow Roman Catholics in other parts of the world.

This principle of Churches which enjoy unity without uniformity may, in the end, turn out to be an important element in future plans for reunion. When interviewed in London in 1964 the present Archbishop of Canterbury, after discussing the barriers between Anglicans and Roman Catholics, said: 'Given the solution of the major dogmatic difficulties – and that's a big presumption – but given that presumption, unity could take the form of the Anglican Communion being in communion with Rome, having sufficient dogmatic agreement with Rome, accepting the Pope as the presiding bishop of all Christendom, but being allowed to have our own liturgy and married clergy and a great deal of existing Anglican customs; that is to say, it would be a position rather like the Eastern Uniat Churches in relation to the See of Rome.'[1]

The fourth barrier is difficult to describe but might, perhaps, be called 'discipline' or 'way of life' or 'moral standards'. To some non-Roman Catholics this sometimes appears as the most formidable barrier of them all. In the Anglican Church, as in many others, much liberty is allowed to the individual. We have very little Canon Law, preferring to act on a few basic principles and leave much to individual judgment and personal choice. Any idea of such things as an 'Index of Prohibited Books' would be ludicrous to us, for we know that we should be unable to agree on its contents or to enforce its use. On the other hand, we have Puritan and Evangelical traditions – such as Sabbatarianism, a dislike of gambling, and, to some people, a disapproval of smoking and drinking – which do not seem to trouble members of the Church of Rome.

The fact that we have practically no Canon Law means that individual cases can be – and, indeed, must be – judged on

[1] *Herder Correspondence*, 1964, pp. 265–6.

their own merits. It is not often that a parish priest or a bishop of the Anglican Church can issue commands, and, if he did, he would have little hope of being obeyed. He must, therefore, act by persuasion, by counsel, trying always to do what is best for the individual soul. I remember a discussion in Rome on the question of admitting to Holy Communion people who had been divorced and remarried, when I was asked what the rules were in the Church of England. My reply was that there were no rules. The Prayer Book says that 'notorious evil livers' shall not be admitted; but a woman who, perhaps largely for the sake of her children, has remarried after being deserted by her first husband, would hardly come into that category. The Prayer Book also lays down three conditions upon which people may approach the altar – that they 'truly, and earnestly repent', are 'in love and charity' with all men, and 'intend to lead a new life following the commandments of God'. I pointed out, there-fore, that if these conditions were observed, if there was sincere penitence for past sins, no bitterness for past wrongs, and a genuine intention of making good, then such a person would be admitted. This would be based on the belief that the sacraments are not rewards for good living, but means of grace, and on the knowledge that Christ said that 'they that are whole need not the physician but they that are sick'.

I then asked what the custom was in the Roman Church, and was told that no one who has been divorced and had remarried could ever receive the sacrament, since the sacrament could not be given to those living in sin. In this case penitence was no good, as absolution could not be given if the woman showed no intention of giving up the sin of living with a man who was not her husband. Unless and until she was prepared to do that, she clearly could not present herself at the altar. Here then were two opposite points of view, one pastoral, the other legal; the only comforting element in the conversation was when another Roman Catholic priest who was present attacked the canonist by saying: 'You care more for Canon Law than you do for the souls of the people.'

I mention this incident because it conveys a real difference of approach to the Church's mission. I believe that the Council will have done something to emphasise the pastoral as against the juridical nature of the Church; but, even so, a lot of adjustment and toleration would be necessary before Churches with such different ideas and methods could be united.

As the Vatican Council has shifted the whole balance of the ecumenical encounter, Anglicans are obliged to take another look at their own future. How is the Council going to affect us? What difference is it likely to make to the various projects in which we have become involved in recent years?

It has been fairly clear for some time that the Anglican Communion will, sooner or later, have to unite with someone. Becoming separated from Rome in the sixteenth century, it became a national Church, the Church of the English people; but, in the course of time, it went where English colonialism went and is now scattered over most parts of the world. Organised in 345 dioceses and 24 provinces, it looks impressive; but its numbers are small compared with other groups. It is also now in process of disintegration. Already the Church of South India has taken off a number of Anglican dioceses, and other plans for unions are moving towards maturity in other parts of the world. In the British Isles the Anglican-Methodist proposals look like bringing the 'Church of England' to an end during the next few years, as the Anglican-Presbyterian plan would mean the demise of the Episcopal Church in Scotland.

To many people – perhaps to most – all this seems not only inevitable, but desirable. Anglicanism, as they know it, has much in common with other reformed communions. Presbyterians and Methodists are our kith and kin. Many are intermarried, or have relations who belong to another ecclesiastical group. Naturally it seems right that those who *can* unite should do so as soon as possible. The difficulties do not appear to be very formidable. A little more charity and effort should do the trick. So at the British Council of Churches Conference at Nottingham in 1964 there was passed, by an overwhelming majority, a resolution that 'united in our urgent desire for One Church Renewed for Mission, this Conference invites the members of the British Council of Churches, in appropriate groupings such as nations, to covenant together to work and pray for the inauguration of union by a date agreed amongst them. We dare to hope that this date should not be later than Easter Day, 1980'.

Here then is a target and a challenge. But even if the goal is reached, and that, by Easter 1980, the member Churches of the British Council of Churches have become united, we shall not necessarily have come any nearer to Christian Unity, nor will the Christians in Great Britain have produced 'one Church renewed for mission'. The policy which lies behind the Nottingham resolution, and behind all the schemes and plans for unions in other parts of the world, could produce no more than one of three Churches, of which one would be the Roman Church (containing half of all the Christians in the world), one would be a possible union of all the Oriental Churches, Orthodox and otherwise, and the third would be the amalgamation of those Churches which may be said to have stemmed from the Reformation. Perhaps something along these these lines is the most that can be hoped for for the next stage in Christian history. But no one could view it with much satisfaction, and many Anglicans dread the disappearance of so much which is dear and important to them. The 'coming great Church' may be 'coming'; but it doesn't look very 'great', since at best it could not contain more than thirty per cent of the Christian population of the world, and would probably be a good deal less.

But if the future of Anglicanism lies not with Protestantism, where does it lie? Some Anglicans naturally turn with hope and expectation towards the Orthodox Churches of the East. Here, they say, is the nearest approach to a primitive and uncorrupted Church, the Church which has produced great scholars and great saints, and which has continued to hold the allegiance of its members through centuries of persecution and danger. Professor Hodges begins his pamphlet, *Anglicanism and Orthodoxy*, with these words:

> 'This paper is written in the belief that the friendly relations which now subsist between the Orthodox Churches and the Anglican Communion ought to be made closer and more intimate, and that the Anglican Churches ought to approximate more and more to Orthodoxy until at last they could be recognised as actual members of the Orthodox family';[1]

and he then goes on, after a study of the Anglican Church, to suggest that the proper future for the Church of England is that it should become the birthplace of 'western Orthodoxy'.

There are, no doubt, some who share Professor Hodges' views and hopes. For those who want Catholicism without Romanism the prospect is attractive. Furthermore, a union of Anglicanism with Orthodoxy would make a strong buffer-state between Roman Catholicism and world Protestantism, a 'third party' with which both of the main parties would wish to be on good terms. But a union of this kind would never win the consent of the majority of Anglicans, since so few of them would either understand or care. They know practically nothing about the Orthodox Church, and what they do know seems utterly remote from their idea of what a Church should be. They may occasionally see a bearded priest in black, flowing robes, stove-pipe hat and veil. They may, perhaps on holiday in Greece, have entered a church where the Liturgy was being performed; but it would seem very strange and totally unlike what they enjoy in

[1] H. A. Hodges, *Anglicanism and Orthodoxy: a Study in Dialectical Churchmanship* (London, 1955), p. 9.

their church at home. An Anglican-Orthodox union could, in fact, come about only if Anglicanism disintegrated. Should this happen (as it may well do), there will no doubt be a group who, refusing to join a conglomeration of reformed Churches, and finding it impossible to submit to Rome, would find their home in Orthodoxy. This might lead to the establishment in the English-speaking world of a 'western Orthodoxy', but it would not contribute much to the cause of Christian Unity.

Realising that any union with Orthodoxy is very remote, Anglicans naturally turn to Churches which are closer at hand – Roman and Protestant. Of the two there is no doubt that Rome presents by far the more serious problem. As a result of national and racial antagonisms, and a long history of persecution and bitterness, all the natural barriers between Rome and other types of Christianity are greatly enlarged. Suspicion, misunderstanding, ignorance, fear, jealousy – all of them would have to be overcome before much progress would be made. And how many would be prepared to make the initial effort?

So Anglicans naturally drift in the opposite direction where they find fellow-Christians who are willing to come half way to meet them. Here union seems so much more possible, especially to those who neither know nor care much about episcopacy, apostolic succession, continuity, tradition, and who probably know very little of what happened between the close of the New Testament and the advent of John Wyclif. So long as they can continue to enjoy the familiar pattern of worship and ministry they are quite happy to enter into organic union with anyone who will leave them alone. So it is assumed by many that a union of the kind envisaged by the Nottingham Conference is the right thing to do; and anyone who expresses any doubt about it is suspected of being a reactionary, a crypto-papist, perhaps even a traitor or at least hopelessly unenlightened and uncharitable, an ecumenical moron.

But perhaps those who cast doubts upon the wisdom of plans

for unions among the little company of the reformed are not
quite as moronic as they look. After all, we talk a lot about
Christian 'Unity', and 'Unity', according to the *Oxford Diction-
ary* means 'one-ness; being one or single or individual; being
formed of parts that constitute a whole'. If there is to be one-
ness among the disciples of Christ, then it must be something
more than a union of the reformed, and must include both
Orthodoxy and Rome.

'The Committee' said the bishops of the Anglican Communion in 1908, 'are not unmindful of the fact that there can be
no fulfilment of the Divine Purpose in any scheme of reunion
which does not ultimately include the great Latin Church of
the West'. This was a remarkable statement, which might have
had great consequences had not the whole question of Christian
unity been directed into a different channel two years later at
Edinburgh. Since then the Anglican Church has been more
and more involved in the problem of union with fellow reformed Churches, and, to a lesser extent, with Orthodoxy. But
now, nearly sixty years later, the question of true Christian
Unity, which involves 'the great Latin Church of the West', as
well as other Christians, has again come to the fore. Whether
we like it or not, we are now obliged to look at the Church of
Rome in a new light. The ecumenical problem in 1966 is quite
different from what it was in 1961. A new pattern has emerged
as a result of the Council, and much of the thought and
language which was valid five years ago is now obsolete.

As we face an entirely new situation, we must adjust our
minds to the new problems and opportunities which lie before
us. First of all, we must see that doors which have been opened
are not shut. Now that the Council is over there is great danger
of inertia, of allowing things to go stale, of slipping back into
the old ways when Rome and the rest of the Christian world
stood so far apart and did so little together. Secondly, we must
be prepared to talk, to listen and to learn. The time for prejudice

nd exclusiveness is over. If the Holy Spirit has induced the Roman Church to make tentative advances towards other Churches, then we must go out to meet her; otherwise, we shall be obstructing the Spirit of God in his work. Thirdly, it is time to take a new look at our own history and our own form-ularies and ask ourselves how much we are to blame for any separation which took place in the past. 'If we are in any way to blame for that separation', said Paul VI, 'we humbly beg God's forgiveness, and ask pardon too of our brethren who feel themselves to have been injured by us'.[1] These thoughts were echoed by the Council fathers who, quoting the words of S. John that 'if we say that we have not sinned . . . his word is not in us', go on to say: 'This holds good for sins against unity. Thus, in humble prayer we beg pardon of God and of our separated brethren, just as we forgive them that trespass against us' (De Ecumenismo, § 7). So far as I know, nothing of a similar nature has come from our side. This is sad, for it will inevitably give the world the impression that charity and forgiveness are characteristic only of the Church of Rome.

It is essential, therefore, that non-Roman Christians should take the Council seriously and try to see it as a real step forward on the road towards Christian Unity. Difficult and humiliating though it may be, we must now look at all our schemes for partial union in the light of possible unity – as the Lambeth fathers urged us to do in 1908. Their wise advice has been largely ignored, but the work of the Council encourages us to look at the problem again. To say that union with Rome is impossible is, first, to deny the power of God 'with whom all things are possible', and, secondly, to write off Christ's high-priestly prayer as unrealistic or as wishful-thinking.

The tragedy is that so much effort in the past fifty years has gone into what, at the best, could affect less than half of the Christian world. For this we are all to blame. But, now that the

[1] X. Rynne, *The Second Session*, p. 358.

ecumenical opportunity has so greatly improved, we shall indeed be held guilty if, through fear or prejudice or any other
sin or weakness, we fail to seize the opportunity which God has
given us of working not just for partial unions but for that
perfect unity in which all are one.

APPENDIX

The following is the text of the address given by Pope Paul VI in the basilica of S. Paul's-without-the-walls on the occasion of the Joint Service on 4 December, 1965. The speech was delivered in French. The translation here given is from *One in Christ* (vol. 2, No. 2, 1966), pp. 162–4.

'Dear Observers, or rather let us call you by the name which has sprung to life again during these four years of the Ecumenical Council: Brothers and Friends in Christ!

Now the Council is drawing to its close and you are going to leave us; we wish, in this moment of farewell, to become the interpreter of the venerable Council Fathers who have come with us this evening, to pray with you and to say good-bye.

Each of you is going back to his own home, and we shall find ourselves alone. Let us share with you this deep impression: your departure will leave a loneliness around us which we knew nothing of before the Council but which now saddens us; we would like to see you with us always!

This obliges us to say once again how grateful we are for your presence at our Ecumenical Council. We have greatly appreciated this presence; we have felt its influence; we have admired its nobility, its piety, its patience, its friendliness. And that is why we shall keep a grateful memory of your coming, and as we think over the courtesy of these human and Christian contacts we shall be able to appreciate more justly the historical significance of the fact of your presence, to discover its religious content and penetrate the mystery of the divine plan which it seems both to hide and to reveal.

And so your departure will not mean for us the end of those cordial spiritual relationships brought to life by your presence at the Council; it will not close for us a dialogue begun in the silence, but on the contrary it will oblige us to study how we can fruitfully pursue it. The friendship will remain. And what will also remain, as the first fruits of the conciliar meeting, is the conviction that the great problem of reunion in the unity of the Church, visible to all those who have the joy and the responsibility of the name of Christians, must be studied in all its depth and that the hour for this is now come. Many of you knew it already; now the number of those who think like this has grown, and that is a great advantage.

If we want to summarize the fruits concerning the question of unity which have ripened on the occasion and because of the Council, we can first of all state the fact of a deepened awareness of the existence of the problem itself: a problem which concerns us all and calls us all. We can add another fruit, yet more precious: the hope that the problem – not today, certainly, but tomorrow – may be resolved; slowly, gradually, loyally, generously. That is a great thing.

And it is the sign that still other fruits have ripened: we have learned to know you a little better, and not only as the representatives of your respective confessions: through your persons we have come into contact with Christian communities which live, pray and act in the name of Christ, with doctrinal systems and religious mentalities, let us say it without fear: with Christian treasures of great value.

Far from making us jealous, this has rather increased in us the sense of brotherhood, and the desire to re-establish between us that perfect communion willed by Christ. And that brings us to discover yet more positive results on the road to peace: we have recognized certain faults and certain mutual feelings that were not good; for the former we have asked pardon of God and of you; with regard to the latter we have discovered their non-Christian roots and have determined, for our part, to transform them into sentiments worthy of the school of Christ; we renounce polemics based on prejudice and full of offence, and we do not seek prestige in vanity; we seek rather to keep in mind the repeated exhortations of the Apostle over whose tomb we meet tonight: not to allow between us "quarelling, jealousy, anger, selfishness, slander, gossip, conceit, and disorder". We want to take up again a relationship which is human, serene, full of goodwill, trustful.

You know the steps which we have tried to take in this direction. It is enough to recall the meetings which through these years the representatives of the Holy See and ourselves have had the honour and the joy to have with so many members of your communities. Of especial significance was the unforgettable interview which Providence accorded us with His Holiness Patriarch Athenagoras at Jerusalem at the beginning of last year; it was followed by other moving visits from representatives of different Christian confessions which for centuries had had no contact with the Catholic Church, and particularly with the Holy See. We consider these fraternal meetings as a historic fact of great importance and we see them as the prelude to the most comforting developments.

But that is not all: you know, Brothers, that our Ecumenical Council has set itself in motion towards you in many ways: from the consideration which the conciliar Fathers have not ceased to show in your presence, which has been so dear to them, to the unanimous effort to avoid any expression which was not full of regard for you; from the spiritual joy of seeing your group, an élite, associated with the religious ceremonies of the Council, to the formulation of doctrinal and disciplinary expressions in a way which would avoid obstacles and open roads as wide and flat as possible, for a better evaluation of the Christian religious heritage which you conserve and develop: the Roman Catholic Church, you see, has demonstrated that she wants to understand you and to be understood; she has pronounced no anathemas but only invitations; she has set no limits to her patient hope, no more than to her fraternal offer to continue a dialogue to which she has committed herself. She would have loved, with Pope John – to whom we owe the fact that we can talk again in trust and brotherhood – to celebrate with you, with some of you, the decisive and final meeting; but she realizes that this is too human a haste, and that before we arrive at a full and authentic communion there still remains a long way to go, many prayers to raise up to the Father of lights, many vigils to keep. At least, as the Council ends, we can record a victory: we have begun to love one another again, and may it be the Lord's pleasure that at least because of this the world may recognize that we are truly his disciples, because we have established mutual love between us once more.

You are going away again. Do not forget that love with which the Roman Catholic Church will continue to think of you and to follow you. Do not believe her to be unfeeling and proud because she feels it her duty to guard jealously the "deposit" which she has carried with her from the beginning, and do not accuse her of having deformed or betrayed this deposit if, in the course of her careful, loving and centuries-old meditation, she has discovered treasures of truth and life whose renunciation would mean unfaithfulness. Think that it is indeed from Paul, the apostle of her ecumenicity, that she received her first training in dogmatic magisterium, and you know with what implacable firmness. And think that truth dominates and liberates us all, and also that truth is near, very near, to love.

We pass on to you, just as it has lingered in our memory, the story of an episode full of grace and symbolism in the life of one of the great Eastern thinkers of the modern age which was told to us many years ago. We think that it refers to Soloviev. He was once in a monastery and had prolonged a spiritual conversation with a pious monk until a late hour. Finally, wishing to return to his cell, he went out into the corridor and was faced by a number of cell doors, all exactly alike and all firmly shut. In the darkness he was not able to identify the door of the cell which had been given to him; and on the other hand it was impossible in the blackness to return to that of the monk whom he had just left, while he had no wish to disturb anyone during the strict monastic silence of the night. Thus the philosopher resigned himself to passing the night in a slow thoughtful walk up and down the corridor of the monastery which had suddenly become so mysterious and inhospitable. The night was long and weary, but finally it came to an end and the first light of dawn meant that the weary philosopher was at last able with no difficulty to identify the door of the cell which he had passed again and again without recognizing it. And this was his commentary: it is often like this for those who seek the truth; they pass very close to it in the course of their long vigils without finding it, until a ray of the sun of the divine wisdom comes to make the comforting discovery as easy as it is happy. The truth is near. Beloved Brothers, may this ray of divine light make us all recognize the blessed door!

That is our desire. And now, on the tomb of Paul, let us pray together.'

After the Joint Service the Pope met the observers in
an adjoining room when the Bishop of Ripon spoke as
follows:

'Your Holiness,

As the Council draws towards its end, I would like, first of all,
to express my thanks, and the thanks of us all, for the opportunity
which we have had of participating in the work of the Council,
and for the warmth of the welcome which has been extended to
us. Some of us were present at the Opening Service of the Council
in October, 1962, when we found that we had been allotted the
best seats of all in the basilica, so that there was no one between
us and Pope John. This act of courtesy, as delightful as it was un-
expected, set the tone for the whole of the Council.

Fot this we know that we owe a deep debt of gratitude to Pope
John XXIII, *felicis memoriae*, and also to Your Holiness. We feel
that, from the very beginning we have been treated as honoured
guests. Never once, in the four years, have we felt any resentment
at our presence. On the contrary, we have always been led to
suppose that our presence has, in more ways than one, contributed
to the success of the Council in the great task to which it has set
its hand.

Our understanding of the work of the Council has been
greatly facilitated by the endless trouble taken by the members
and staff of the Secretariat for Promoting Christian Unity under
the leadership of our good friends Cardinal Bea and Bishop
Willebrands. Equally grateful are we to the translators, who have
patiently sat with us each day and helped us in our stumbling,
and often unsuccessful, efforts to understand the Latin as spoken
with so many different accents.

For all of this we are deeply thankful, and would like Your
Holiness to know that when we leave Rome next week we shall
carry with us very happy memories of our sojourn here as your
honoured guests.

The Council is drawing to its end; but the work for Christian
Unity is but beginning. We outside the communion of the Roman
Church have for long been occupied in prayer, in dialogue and in
effort for the union of our respective Churches. Now, with the

entry of the Roman Catholic Church into this field, we realise that the Ecumenical Movement has taken on a new dimension. At last we can say that the whole Christian world is engaged in the search for that unity for which Our Blessed Lord prayed.

We know, of course, that Unity – in which all are one – is not something to be easily or quickly achieved. We know that it will require much wisdom, much patience, much faith, hope and charity, on the part of us and of those who will follow us. But we believe that the days of mutual fear, of rigid exclusiveness and of arrogant self-sufficiency, on either side, are passing away. The road to Unity will indeed be long and difficult; but it may be of comfort to Your Holiness to know that, as a result of our presence here as Observers, you will have a company of more than a hundred men, all of whom have, at one time or another, been present at the Council, who, as they go all over the world, will try to carry to the Churches something of the spirit of friendship and tolerance which they have seen in the aula of S. Peter's. Our work as Observers is not done. I would like you, dear Holy Father, to think of us as your friends – and, indeed, as your messengers – as we go our respective ways.

In speaking about the Council I have always said that all that the Council has achieved has been helpful to us, both in the positive sense of what has been declared, and in the negative sense of what has been avoided. This I believe to be true; and I am sure my fellow-observers will agree with me. The decree on Ecumenism, the Constitution on the Church, the declaration on Religious liberty, and the decree on the Missionary Activity of the Church together form a basis on which future dialogue and co-operation can proceed. For these we are deeply thankful.

But may I express the hope that, having done so much, the Church of Rome will be willing to go further and do her best to take away, so far as she can, those barriers which still remain between us, and which are such serious obstacles to the attainment of unity.

As the Council concludes its work, and its members are scattered to the four corners of the earth, we realise how great is the burden which rests upon your shoulders, Holy Father, in the difficult days which lie ahead. I think we understand something of the problems which you have to face since you were elected to the chair of S. Peter. We know that those problems will always be with you.

May I, then, assure you that those of us who have worked with you here, and many others who care for the future of the Christian Church, will continue to pray, with all our hearts, that God will guide and strengthen you in your difficult and lonely task.

I conclude with the words of S. Paul to the Philippians: *Gratia vobis et pax a Deo Patre nostro et Domino Iesu Christo. Gratias ago Deo meo in omni memoria vestri . . . confidens hoc ipsum, quia qui coepit in vobis opus bonum perficiet usque in diem Christi Iesu.*'